Anger and Conflict Management

Personal Handbook

Gerry Dunne, Ph.D.

with Dennis Alberson, LCSW

This *Personal Handbook* has been developed for the participants in Anger and Conflict Management Classes and for independent use without the class. An *Anger and Conflict Management: Leader's Guide*, providing a structured format for a ten-hour class as well as outreach guidelines, is also available for counselors and trainers. Participants in these classes utilize their copies of this corresponding *Personal Handbook*.

Personal Handbooks may be purchased as single books or in quantity at a discount. To obtain copies of these publications, contact Personhood Press. Contact the author, through the publisher, regarding a customized Anger and Conflict Management class for your staff or for training of trainers in your organization.

Personhood Press
P.O. Box 1185
Torrance, CA 90505
(800) 662-9662
personhoodpress@att.net

A special thanks to Dennis Alberson, LCSW, who offered numerous scenarios and interpretations for this handbook based on his many years of counseling experience with adults and teens.

Cover art and logos by Linda Jean Thille.
Interior graphics and layout by Lori Bouslaugh.

ISBN: 1-932181-09-1

Published in the United States of America

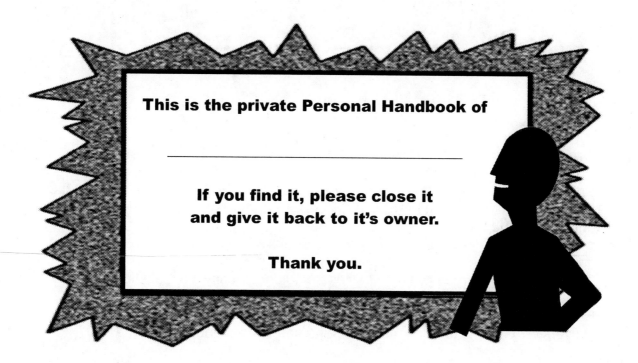

This is the private Personal Handbook of

_____

If you find it, please close it
and give it back to it's owner.

Thank you.

A resident of Battle Ground, Washington, Gerry earned a Bachelor of Arts Degree at Chapman University in Orange, California, a Master of Science Degree at the University of Southern California, Los Angeles, and a Ph.D. in Psychology at the Saybrook Institute in San Francisco. She has served as a classroom teacher, university professor, publisher, business woman, counselor and trainer/consultant to a wide variety of organizations. She has authored and published over 20 manuals and texts including *Preventing Violence in Our Schools* (Jalmar Press, Carson, CA). Currently, Gerry serves two universities as adjunct faculty, consults, counsels, and teaches classes in Anger and Conflict Management. Awards include Outstanding Faculty at National University in San Diego and Alumnus of the Year, Chapman University. Gerry is married, has two sons and two grandchildren.

Contents

Guiding Principles
For participants in an Anger and Conflict Management class

Everyone is affected by many types and degrees of anger--our own and the anger of others. It is a powerful emotion and a sensitive subject. Anger deserves our attention, investigation, respect and careful handling.

In class we will foster:
* Safety
* Respect
* Dignity
* Understanding
* Empathy
* Support
* Friendship
* Laughter and Enjoyment

We will avoid:
* Guilt
* Blaming
* Uncomfortable confessions
* Prying
* Ranting
* Gossip
* Put downs

As we investigate anger let's honor these ground rules:

1. Everyone is welcome to speak during class and in small group discussions--to share feelings and opinions, and to ask questions.
2. We will share only those personal experiences we feel comfortable sharing.
3. No one will ever be forced to speak. Listening is a contribution.
4. We will always listen to the person who is speaking.
5. We will do our best to share speaking times equally.
6. We will not interrupt, pry, or put each other down in any way.
7. We will not gossip (no naming names) in class or outside of class.

> **This class is not meant to take the place of professional counseling or therapy. If you have persistent destructive thoughts about yourself or someone else, please seek professional advice.**

"Emotions are the prime movers," intoned my Psychology professor, who went on to explain: *"everything, I mean* everything, *we do relates to our feelings in one way or another."* This idea was both astounding and liberating to me. I was in my early twenties and trying to figure myself out. I wanted to understand other people better too, but my personal motivations and behavior remained my own biggest mystery. *"Of course,"* I said to myself, *"that explains it. How come I never realized how important my feelings were before?"*

I was one of those people who grew up in a family that denied not only the importance of feelings, but usually feelings themselves, especially uncomfortable ones. Emotions were rarely admitted as evidence to anyone's statement of need or search for the truth. If a rare circumstance occurred and a feeling was mentioned ("We forgot to include Sammy and now his feelings are hurt") it was usually done in a depreciated way. The undertone would be: "Oh well, it's just a feeling. Buck up, Sam."

My parents and their contemporaries had been through the depression and as a result had a completely practical, show me, don't-bother-me-with-nonsense attitude toward life. If you wanted to lay an egg in our household you stated feelings like hurt, fear or anger. The folks would look at you as if you'd announced that a comet had landed on the roof and then smirk and look away. This was often true even of my mother who was a kind and loving person at heart.

Instead of stating feelings and discussing them, the tone of our household was a stifled calm (which was actually pretty boring). Then out of nowhere an episode would occur. Tempers blew, terrible things were said, loud hysterical arguments went on sometimes for hours and then it would be over. The silence that resulted would often last for days until the "normal" calm returned as if the blow-up had never happened.

I was usually a witness in these shattering disruptions and occasionally a target. Like everyone else in the family I experienced everything and understood nothing. I was part of the action and part of the denial afterward. As I grew up I fell into one mystifying and painful trap after another with people at school, work, and in my own home because of my ignorance about feelings, especially anger. As a young adult I found to my horror that at times I was the one who offended others and other times it was me who flew off the handle and went out of control.

Just as it was in my childhood home, angry episodes during most of my life have meant temporary, but full-blown insanity of the darkest order. I found that even though the madness would be absent for a time, it could not be eliminated. Anger would surface at the strangest times and I never, ever welcomed it.

I'm still deeply affected by anger, but gradually have become more at ease with it. I noticed that I wasn't the only one who struggled with anger. Everyone seemed to be annoyed about something at one point or another. I also noticed that some people command attention and respect when angry by the way they handle themselves and others expose themselves as vulnerable, weak and even ridiculous when upset. Still others are clearly dangerous. Have you noticed these differences too?

As time went by I got some good help. I enrolled in psychology classes and at length gained a Ph.D. in Developmental Psychology which focuses on how people are affected by their experiences as they navigate through each stage of life. I also read numerous useful books (see the resources at the back of this handbook) and worked with experienced counselors.

These steps gradually led me to reach conclusions about anger that worked for me and I began to develop some strategies for managing it. I became more honest with myself and self-controlling. Instead of repressing my anger and swallowing it, I admitted the hurt or fear that I converted into anger. I also stopped denying the unpleasant reasons for my feelings. Before blowing up or ranting where such impulsive actions would create negative consequences for myself, I got better at letting off steam in ways I wouldn't regret later. Being honest with myself and taking control of myself were not easy but as I met these challenges I became stronger.

I realized that I didn't have to allow someone to hurt me with hostile abuse because that person was really mad at someone else so I flatly said so to the individual and refused to say more. That was another assertive step to righteously protecting myself and managing anger and I felt stronger.

At a certain point I stopped making excuses or ignoring someone who had a legitimate complaint about something I had done to offend him or her. I listened and realized that, yes, the person was right: I'd done it. I faced myself. If he or she had done it to me I would be just as mad, probably madder. It took a lot of nerve but I started admitting my poor behavior in these situations and apologizing. How surprised I was that doing so brought pardon and respect from the people I offended. In almost every case we became better friends and I grew stronger.

The first time I decided to use my anger to energize myself to do something necessary that I preferred to avoid, I felt the tremendous *positive* power in anger. I consciously experienced first hand that energy which all of us can take advantage of for our own benefit, or to help someone else. Knowing this is like taking a healthy breath of air in the real world. Knowing

that I never have to be a victim of anyone's anger, including my own, is a lesson I'm still learning. But consciously working on it continues to make me stronger.

Many of these lessons and management strategies had to be learned over and over again. As a child I had been scarred by painful events caused by out-of-control anger. At that time I was not exposed to many people who understood it or how to use it constructively. But my personal struggles have resulted in some helpful information and insights to share with you. That's what this *Personal Handbook* is about. I hope it will be as helpful for you to use as it has been for me to write.

Anger: Feel It and Channel It!

Managing anger takes honesty, courage and strength! In this handbook we will learn about its forms, dangers, and possibilities for usefulness! We will strive to develop the ability to decide how to channel our anger into constructive actions instead of blindly and impulsively reacting with behavior that may be destructive. We will learn ways to respond skillfully to the anger of others. Our ultimate goal is to empower ourselves to develop our own internal guidelines and begin new habits for controlling and using anger instead of letting it control and use *us!*

The stories, ideas and exercises in this handbook are based on the following concepts and ideas:

- Anger is a normal internal feeling usually experienced as a reaction to an external situation or event.

- Everyone has a right to feel anger, including times when someone's anger is in response to something *you* have done.

- The feeling of anger may spur behavior that is unproductive and destructive or productive and constructive. The feeling and the behavior are not the same.

- Different people feel differently about the same situation or event. Understanding this is the basis for acceptance and respect for oneself and others.

- Each of us has our own unique set of "anger triggers."

- Anger generally comes from hurt, fear, anxiety or grief and often its unmanaged expression causes more hurt, fear, anxiety and grief.

- People tend to imitate others they spend time with. Family members are prime examples. Anger-driven reactions are often unexamined imitations of another person's typical behavior.

- Angry responses to situations are sometimes appropriate, justified and rational. Other times they are inappropriate, unjustified and irrational. Perception and judgement of the situation based on past experiences make the difference.

- The ability to recognize one's anger, and to think about it, allows people to "talk with themselves" and make rational decisions regarding how to channel and use their anger.

5

- Repressing anger within oneself is not healthy because it only remains hidden until something happens to cause it to express itself in behavior. Often this expression is overblown and/or unfairly displaced on someone, or something, other than the actual cause of the anger. Physical and emotional problems can also result when anger is not acknowledged and held inside.

- Anger exists to provide energy which can be used for useful purposes such as protecting the people we love, including ourselves.

- Some of the most unfortunate, destructive expressions of anger occur in homes between family members.

- Anger is easily generated or diminished simply by the way people communicate with each other.

- The messages people send themselves (self-talk), when respectful of self and others, are crucially important elements in managing anger.

- The assertive style of thinking and acting is the basis for anger management.

- Conflicts between individuals and groups can be managed by using a number of strategies that have been proven effective.

Chapter One:
How Does Your Own Anger Affect You?

What makes you angry? Write a list.

_____

_____

_____

_____

_____

_____

_____

_____

_____

_____

_____

Run out of room? Turn to page 22.

Count them. How many things did you list?_____

Identify your degrees of anger.

Look at your list and put a 5 in front of the things that make you maddest (furious, full of rage, incensed). Put a 4 beside the things that make you plenty upset (but not quite at the level of 5). Continue in this manner with 3, 2 and 1, which is the number to put in front of those things that only irritate you to a mild degree.

How many statements did you put a 5 in front of _____ 4____ 3____ 2____ and 1 ____?

You may discover that you are intensely angry about most of the things you listed, not that angry at all or somewhere in between.

How do you experience anger?

What images or forces come to mind when you reflect on your angry feelings?
(Volcanoes, electrical power surges, etc.) Make a list:

_____

_____

_____

_____

_____

_____

Is anger bad?

Think about a time when you became angry. Afterward, how did you feel about
yourself?

_____

_____

_____

_____

_____

_____

Anger happens!

Many people have bad feelings about themselves when they feel angry or just
afterward. They do their best to avoid anger or deny it when it happens. But anger
is not bad--or good; it just is. Guilt, embarrassment, and shame are unhelpful
feelings about your own anger. The fact is that you feel what you feel. *What you
do with your anger is what matters!*

**Accepting anger is the first step in taking charge of it.
(This takes honesty.)**

L👀k back at yourself!

Bring to mind a situation you are proud of. Describe a time when you became angry and handled yourself well so that you didn't get hurt and no one else did either. This might have even been a time when the outcome was great for everyone, not just okay. Write about the angry feelings you felt, what you thought to yourself, what you did, and how things turned out.

_____

_____

_____

_____

_____

_____

_____

_____

_____

_____

What happens to your brain and body when you get mad?

If you were able to remember a time when you became angry and handled it well in the last exercise, you used a part of your intelligence, an ability humans have that other animals don't. (It is true, however, that many humans don't often use this ability and many animals handle difficult situations well without it.)

Before describing this ability, let's look at what all animals, including us, have in common when it comes to upsetting or threatening situations. All living creatures from tiny one-cell organisms to human beings want to stay alive and remain safe. But now let's talk specifically about people.

The moment we perceive, or imagine, a possible threat to our survival or safety, our cerebral cortex sends an alarm signal to the hypothalamus which stimulates the sympathetic nervous system to release the hormone, adrenaline, and send it to our vital body systems. This occurs in order to give us the power to take one of two survival actions: fight or flight. (Freezing on the spot is a third possibility.) Have you ever become suddenly frightened, stressed to the max with mounting irritations, or become extremely angry and felt drained and exhausted afterward?

That's because your brain understands that the threat or danger is gone and stops sending the alarm. In three minutes we usually return to normal but before that our quick and heavy flow of adrenaline has literally drained us.

Walter B. Cannon, a physiologist at Harvard Medical School, first described this "fight or flight" response to threat during the early twentieth century. Later, an endocrinologist, Hans Selye studied this response and discovered exactly what happens in the brain and body when it is experienced. It's a split-second chain reaction shown in this simple diagram:

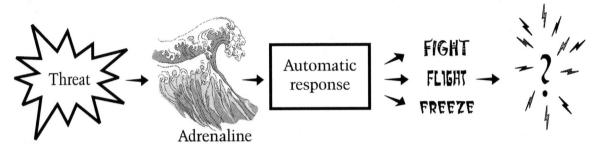

*Notice the question mark at the end which is meant to show an *unknown outcome*.

First, our "animal instincts" take over and we do what is necessary to stay alive. The fight choice is the right one if self-defense is actually necessary. Flight is the correct choice if we have to get away quickly from real danger. And freezing is best if we are safest by staying perfectly still. All of these will result in an outcome which could set the chain reaction going again.

Most of the threats we face don't endanger our lives and limbs, however. They threaten our sense of security or self worth causing appropriate anger. Other threats hassle us, scare us, make us worry, grieve us, hurt us, and disappoint us and we often convert these feelings into anger as well. Why? Because anger feels better than anxiety, grief, hurt and disappointment. It takes away weak feelings and replaces them with an emotion that feels powerful. But complications set in when the normal feeling of anger enters the chain reaction because the automatic response, *fight,* easily takes over and often leads to an undesirable outcome where the question mark is shown on the diagram. Frequently the undesirable outcome leads to new chain reactions with outcomes that are even worse. Later, we wonder how things got so out-of-hand. We ask ourselves, "Why did I say that?" or "Why didn't I just keep my cool?"

Another undesirable outcome is "swallowing" our anger and then forgetting we did so. Numerous medical studies have shown that people who repress their anger again and again are more prone to become ill and depressed than those who express their anger in some way. It's like swallowing poison which stays in the system and becomes more dangerous as time goes by.

The part of our intelligence, the ability we have that other animals don't, is always available to us. We can *choose* to use this ability to "check in" with ourselves anytime to see how we are feeling, to evaluate circumstances and situations, and to *make conscious decisions* for how to use the energy anger gives us for handling ourselves in constructive ways. As we continue to learn how to do this and what strategies to use for handling difficult situations, let's start off by finding out more about the nature of anger and how it operates.

Understanding the Difference between Appropriate and Inappropriate Anger

It's easy to see in others: sometimes people get upset for "righteous," justifiable reasons. At other times they get upset for "just plain crazy" reasons. But this is not so easy to recognize in ourselves. The difference between appropriate and inappropriate anger lies in how a situation is perceived and understood. Clear, present-time reality perception of a provoking situation usually leads to appropriate anger. (Examples might be complete indignation for getting balled out for something you didn't do, or for getting a ticket for speeding when you, in fact, were not speeding.)

Inappropriate anger occurs when perception and thinking are distorted in some way usually by re-experiencing unpleasant feelings from something similar that happened in the past. (Examples: the person who got balled out for something he didn't do might cuss at the brother of the person who balled him out and feel hateful toward anyone in that family. The person who got a bogus ticket might become incensed and start yelling and pounding on the steering wheel the next time she sees a policeman.)

Inappropriate anger that is blown way out of proportion to the actual circumstances is generally caused by other deeper feelings we have already mentioned. Like a volcano with deep forces of hot magma inside, we have forces like hurt, fear, anxiety, disappointment and grief below the surface. These deeper feelings result from deprivations or painful events, sometimes traumatic ones, that happened at an earlier time. *Inappropriate anger has a way of feeling like it's appropriate and that can lead to big problems.*

When a new situation resembling the old one occurs we sometimes "believe" that the same bad thing is happening again and we are prone to "become" the age we were when the old situation occurred. For example, you might become inappropriately angry and feel like a deprived, victimized child when someone eats in front of you and doesn't offer to share (and you are hungry), if you were often punished for misdeeds as a child by not getting to eat dinner with the family.

11

Elements in new situations like the elements in upsetting old situations are often referred to as "anger triggers" because they spark the inappropriate upset. When "triggered" in this way people often react without thinking sensibly. Instead, their thoughts "feed" the bad feelings. They are apt to say things like this to themselves: "I *knew* he didn't really love me!" "Here I am again doing all the work myself with no help." "It's no fair. I always get the blame." These kinds of thoughts go with the hurt or frightened feelings creating justification in the minds of these people for their overblown anger. Next, they are likely to act out and create more aggravation or pout by holding in dangerous, festering resentment. Later they might think the situation over and realize they acted like belligerent, injured children and wonder why they got so upset. If they pouted, they might develop a headache and ask themselves what caused it.

Has anything like this ever happened to you?

_____

_____

_____

_____

_____

_____

_____

_____

_____

_____

_____

_____

_____

_____

_____

_____

_____

_____

You be the judge!

Here are three scenarios. Read each one and decide if the anger each person feels is appropriate or inappropriate by checking on the line of your choice.

John felt furious at his friend, George, because George got sick the day they were going to go fishing.

John's anger is: _____ appropriate _____ inappropriate

Can't decide? Here is some more information: When John was small his parents frequently promised to take him to exciting places. Then they would often drink heavily the night before and have hangovers the next day. When this happened they told John the trip was off because they were sick. When George called John to tell him he wasn't well, John said to himself: "I should have *known* it wouldn't happen. You can't count on anybody."

Annette felt rage at her sister, Liz, when Liz told Annette's boyfriend how cute Annette used to be when she was little and first beginning to talk.

Annette's rage is: _____ appropriate _____ inappropriate

Can't decide? Annette's family speaks French as well as English so when she was little Annette sometimes used a French word in a sentence she'd begun in English. She also lisped. The family got a big kick out of the lisping and language errors and constantly made fun of her. They even laughed and pointed out her mistakes in front of visitors. When Liz talked with Annette's boyfriend about it, Annette's thoughts were: "I hate her. None of them are happy unless I do something stupid to make them laugh."

Harold was extremely disappointed with his wife, Sue, when he came home from work and she wasn't there. Sue had promised to be ready to go out to dinner but she didn't leave a note or call. She showed up three hours later. She didn't apologize, explaining that she "got carried away" at the mall and lost track of time.

Harold's extreme disappointment is: _____ appropriate _____ inappropriate

Can't decide? During Harold's life he has worried people and has been worried by others in this same way. But now, Harold makes it a point to keep his promises and when he is going to be late he leaves a note or calls. Harold has asked Sue to do the same but now and then Sue worries him in this way. Before she came home Harold said to himself: "Something happened to detain her and it could be bad, or she's being inconsiderate again. Either way I don't like it."

Past Hurts Come Back!

It's easy to understand why John, Annette and Harold became upset. Yet when all of the factors leading to their feelings and thoughts are considered it becomes clear that in one case (Harold's) the feelings were appropriate and justified. (Harold felt very bad but did not become enraged.) In the two other cases we find that the feelings of fury and rage are inappropriate because they are based on past hurts. Both John and Annette were extremely upset and "fed" their upsets with negative thoughts. They felt the same awful feelings in full force that they experienced at earlier times in their lives when similar things happened.

What else causes inappropriate anger?

Many causes exist for inappropriate anger, however three others are worth looking at. (The first two are similar to "past hurts" but are different variations.)

Gunnysacking

This happens when someone silently collects irritations and slights until "the last straw is placed on them" causing an overblown reaction. An example is a teen who becomes infuriated and blows her top when a friend teases her about her shirt as they walk home from school together. The shirt was splattered with paint in art class and throughout the day one student after another made a joke about it. During the day the art student suffered the jokes in silence. She "gunnysacked" them. Her friend's remark was the last straw.

Does gunnysacking sound familiar? When have you seen this in someone else or felt it within yourself?

_____

_____

_____

_____

_____

_____

_____

_____

Acting on Habit

This is a behavior pattern that occurs when someone automatically "plugs in" an angry feeling in response to certain situations because "when things like this happen I always get mad." An example is the driver who becomes extremely angry and rants and raves whenever he comes up on someone he believes is driving too slowly.

Does this type of anger sound familiar? When have you seen this in someone else or felt it within yourself?

_____

_____

_____

_____

_____

_____

_____

_____

Having Unrealistic Expectations

When something hoped for doesn't happen most people become understandably disappointed and possibly angry. That's appropriate. But it is inappropriate to become extremely angry on top of disappointment when *expected* things don't happen when those things are one's own unrealistic ideas or fantasies. An example is the child who asked for, and began to expect, an expensive gift for Christmas when his father had recently been laid off from his job. When the expectation was not met the child was very put out and whined all day.

Does anger that happens in this way sound familiar? When have you seen this in someone else or felt it within yourself?

_____

_____

_____

_____

_____

Self Honesty Time!

Try to identify some things that make you inappropriately angry. Go back to the list you made of things that make you angry at the beginning of this chapter, on page 7. Draw a circle around those causes of anger that you realize your angry reactions to are partly, or totally, inappropriate. (Hint: if you put a 5 beside something you know bothers you so much because of past circumstances or something you are kidding yourself about, that might be one to circle.)

Next, write down the deeper emotion next to some of the things that make you angry on your list. For example, if you listed anger at reckless drivers the deeper emotion is probably fear because reckless drivers are dangerous and could hurt you. If you listed rude people your deeper feeling is probably hurt because rudeness is an affront to your self-esteem.

Finally, pick one item you circled and describe why it's on the list and why your feelings about it are inappropriate. If you find none, good for you. But think some more and see if there aren't some things that upset you beyond reason and add them to the list. (Note: this is only honest self-talk, not a time for blaming yourself or feeling guilty. Remember feelings themselves are not good or bad, right or wrong. And, if you can do this, you are proving your honesty, courage and strength to yourself.)

_____

_____

_____

_____

_____

_____

_____

_____

_____

_____

> ★ **Recognizing when your anger is appropriate and inappropriate, and being able to "talk with yourself" honestly about it, is the second step in taking charge of it. (This takes courage.)** ★

L👀k back at yourself again.

Fortunately, everyone has the ability to grow and change. We can learn from the feelings we felt and the things we did in the past and evaluate them. Think back to a situation that angered you that you would feel differently about, and react to differently, if it happened now. (You might even be angrier.) Describe the situation, how you felt and reacted, and how you would feel and react at this point.

_____

_____

_____

_____

_____

_____

_____

L👀k to the Future!

The more aware and accepting you become of your feelings, and the more you are able to honestly talk with yourself about whether they are appropriate or not, the more you can choose constructive actions. These are actions that will not make things worse for you or anyone else. Because anger is such a powerful emotion, positive actions you intend to take are likely to bring very good results.

Think about an upcoming event or situation that's bound to occur such as a holiday with relatives. Describe your feelings about it honestly. (It's okay if some of your feelings are inappropriate. That's normal. What you need to do is realize it.) Then describe the constructive actions you resolve to take:

_____

_____

_____

_____

_____

_____

_____

17

> **The final step to becoming in charge of yourself
> is resolving to act constructively,
> no matter how you feel.
> (This takes strength.)**

 HOMEWORK: If you haven't read the short story, *"Emotions are the Prime Movers..."* an introduction to your handbook on pages 3 and 4, go back and read it now. Did you skip any of the sections in this chapter? Find them and re-read the ones you skipped. If you left any of the spaces blank, write answers to those questions.

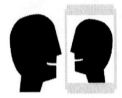 **LIFE WORK:** Before going to the next chapter step back into life. For about a week watch what happens around you and watch people's reactions. See what causes them to become angry and try to tell if their anger is appropriate or inappropriate. Do the same with yourself. In the next chapter you will have a short quiz about these two types of anger. You will also get a chance to examine how angry feelings are handled in your family.

"Have you heard the one about the puzzled new husband?" a friend asked me.

The story went like this: a newly married couple invited the bride's parents and grandmother to dinner shortly after they were married. Having decided to prepare a roast, the bride cut the end off before placing it in the pan. This puzzled her new husband who inquired, "Why did you do that?"

"Well, ... I don't know," answered his wife, "My mom always cut the end off the roasts she fixed and I never asked her why."

That evening shortly after the older folks arrived, the new husband asked his mother-in-law why she cut the end off her roasts before placing them in the pan. Her answer: "Well, ... I don't know. My mother always did that so I just did it too."

Everyone's eyes turned to the grandmother who broke out in a huge grin. "I suppose all of you want to know why I cut the end off *my* roasts?" she asked. "So, I'll tell you. I had a small pan and I had to cut the ends off my roasts to get them to fit!"

This funny story stuck in my mind and caused me to reflect on some of my own family's traditions and habits that passed from one generation to the next. A variety of memories came up, some heart-warming, some strange, and one I didn't really want to think about because it was extremely painful. The memory I wish I could erase from my mind was actually a blur of recollections centered around the explosive anger my father frequently unleashed on my younger brother, Bobby Jim.

My first recollection of such an explosion is very clear. It occurred when I was about four and Bob (as I call him now) was two. My mother had been painting her fingernails with bright red polish, which intrigued us both. We begged her to paint our fingernails too. Later, when my father came home, I ran to show him my nails and received a few complimentary words. Then Bob did the same thing saying, "Look at my pretty nails too, Daddy!"

Without hesitating my father shocked us all by bellowing, "You little sissy! No son of mine wears that stuff. Don't you know any better? Get your mother to take it off right now!"

Bob and I both burst into tears at this unexpected outburst, but it was Bob who got another helping of my father's disdain, "Yeah, go on. Be a big baby. What kind of a boy are you, crying like that? Keep it up and I'll give you something to cry about."

Convulsing at this point, Bob couldn't stop crying. Our Dad didn't hit him with his hand but tore at him with terrible curses and more words of ridicule. Totally shaken, I hid myself in the back of my closet and stayed there for hours. Bob probably did something similar. As I recall, neither of us could eat our dinners. We crept into our beds that night with few words to each other or to our parents.

It took days for our home to return to "normal" which confused my father. Glowering at us he loudly asked mother, "What's the matter with you and the kids?" No one seemed to know how to put into words what the matter was because we were at a loss. Thus began a pattern that repeated itself in our family many, many times and lasted for almost two decades. Does it remind you of anything you have experienced or heard about?

My mother and I were horrified when these events took place. Where this terrible fury within my father came from mystified me and I felt utterly helpless to do anything to stop it. One time I approached my father and asked in a child's primitive way for him to please be nicer to Bobby. He smiled at me and told me I was sweet to love my brother so much but that I was being silly. Clearly, Daddy had no comprehension of how destructive his actions were nor how serious my plea. Between his bouts of fury my father was "a regular guy" who was generous and fun to be around. He liked to take us for rides to the beach or the mountains and had a gift for telling hilariously funny stories.

Occasionally I was the target of Daddy's ire but when that happened it was never with the intensity that exploded all over my poor brother who became severely asthmatic by the time he was three. To make matters worse, my father constantly compared us during our childhood to illustrate Bob's shortcomings. "Why can't you be like your sister?" he'd ask. "She manages to get good grades, finish her homework, get her chores done, make friends, stay clean and neat, etc." No matter what it was I was better at it than he was. Completely overlooked were the facts that I was two years older than Bob and not burdened with serious illness. No wonder my brother frequently expressed bitter feelings toward me and we often fought. For years we were not close after going into our own separate lives.

There was no way I could have known during those early years what I learned later about my own father's victimized childhood and the pit of pain and fear he endured as a youngster. It all began just before the turn of the century. My father's father was an uneducated, but charming, Irish immigrant who won the affection and hand of my German grandmother, a well-educated governess to the children of an important aristocratic family in California. After marrying, my grandparents had four children; my father was the youngest. Tragically, his mother died when he was born. Not knowing how to raise the children himself, my grandfather placed all of them in an institution. If it hadn't been for my caring Aunt Glory, his sister who was ten-years old at the time of her mother's death, my father would have surely died of neglect. When Daddy was four-years old a strange man (his father) came for the children along with his new wife to take them home. But life actually became worse for my father after that because, for reasons no one ever knew, his stepmother despised him. She frequently goaded her husband into whipping the boy.

I'll never forget the evening my father told me all this. I was in my twenties as I listened to the shocking story. "Those whippings were beatings with a leather strap and it happened a lot," my Dad said with tears in his eyes. "I've tried to forget it but I just can't. My Dad would get drunk and come looking for me. He beat me so bad I could hardly walk afterward. Once I was in bed for days. I tried not to cry when he beat me but if I did he'd hit me harder with the strap and call me a bloody sissy." During the same conversation my dad told me, "I've tried to be a good father to you kids. I didn't want to be like my old man so I never beat you."

How revealing! In his own mind my father believed he had been a better father than his father had been and technically he was right. His psychological abuse of my brother seemed like nothing to him compared to the physical abuse he received from *his* Dad. From one generation to the next the pattern did continue but there was improvement.

20

After I became a mother with two little boys of my own, my mother told me about an incident that took place between my father and my sons when they were four and six-years old. My parents were babysitting and during the visit at their house four-year old Danny hurt himself and began to cry.

Mother described how my father's standard response of disgust to a boy's tears became triggered.

"What's the matter with you?" he thundered. "Don't be such a baby. Big boys don't cry."

Danny considered my dad and with great dignity responded, "It's all right to cry, Grampa. Crying makes you feel better." Then Ricky his older brother, added, "Yeah. It's not bad to cry, Grampa."

"What did Daddy say to that?" I asked with delight.

Mother's eye's twinkled. "Not a word," she answered. "It stopped him in his tracks. He just looked at them and then walked away scratching his head." According to her my dad probably never understood how expressing hurt and anger could be healthy, but he never unfairly scolded or ridiculed another grandchild from that day on.

We started at a low point, but from one generation to the next, our family *is* getting better. I was pleased with Ricky and Danny's response to their grandfather. It's also good to be able to tell you that my brother, Bob, never abused his children, not with hands and not with words. He and I have finally become close friends and have grandchildren of our own. To our great joy this latest generation is being nurtured with love and respect.

Notes:

Chapter Two:
Anger and Family Dynamics

Anger is a Natural Emotion!

By itself it's neither good nor bad and someone who feels anger is not a good or bad person when having the feeling. *What counts is the manner in which anger is acted upon.*

Anger is a feeling that powers actions! Without conscious direction from the brain for how to use it, it can be like an exploding grenade going off in all directions and lacerating the one holding it and other people nearby. When anger is repressed and the person won't let him/herself feel it or deal with it, the anger could be like an underwater mine just waiting for one of its spikes to get touched. When it goes off, or leaks, it damages the person's insides more than it damages anyone or anything else. However, when people are honest with themselves, and know they are angry and decide to use the anger to help them achieve an honorable goal, the anger can be like an amazing power tool or a laser that does a precision job.

It bears repeating: the anger we feel can be appropriate (rational, justified, righteous) or inappropriate (irrational, unjustified and unrighteous). Appropriate anger is anger anyone would feel in reaction to a provoking situation. Inappropriate anger is overblown for the situation at hand. We all experience both kinds but it is much easier to identify inappropriate anger in someone else than in ourselves because inappropriate anger "feels" appropriate when we're experiencing it.

Take a look at your own anger over the past week:

Have you observed yourself having the experience of appropriate anger?
Write about the cause and the level of anger you experienced, 5, 4, 3, 2, or 1?

_____

_____

_____

_____

_____

Time out for a True or False Quiz

True___ False___ 1. When your anger is appropriate you can act constructively or destructively.

True___ False___ 2. When your anger is inappropriate you can act constructively or destructively.

True___ False___ 3. When you are appropriately angry it is easier to act constructively than it is when you are inappropriately angry.

True___ False___ 4. When you are inappropriately angry it is harder to act constructively than it is when you are appropriately angry.

If you marked all four of the items true you aced the quiz. Inappropriate anger is the hardest of the two types to channel into constructive actions. It's important to know when you are inappropriately angry whenever possible so you can carefully choose what to do instead of acting on impulse or destructive habit.

When Anger Happens in Families

For most people there's no other people, or ongoing set of circumstances, that can emotionally affect us as powerfully as our families. When people live with each other and have a history between them they will inevitably bother and disappoint each other. Even within the most harmonious families people frequently rub each other the wrong way.

Inappropriate anger happens a lot in families because it is so easy to mix up the past with the present, to gunnysack, to act on habit, and have unreasonable expectations with family members. That we care about our parents, kids, siblings, grandparents and other relatives makes it even more complicated and difficult. *We want them to act the way we want them to act!*

Sometimes we're generous and loving and other times we find ourselves being deeply offended, acting like brats, trying to control everyone else or saying and doing things we wish later we could take back or undo. Sadly, many people are more likely to find themselves hurting, and being hurt by, the people in their families than by anyone else.

Let's take a closer look:

Destructive actions spurred by both appropriate and inappropriate anger can occur anywhere but most often they happen in homes between family members. *When these actions occur thinking is not rational but takes a shortsighted left turn into justifying the destructive behavior.* Here are some examples:

Unconscious Imitation: As we grow up we are strongly influenced in thousands of ways by our parents and other family members including how to respond when hurt, fearful or annoyed. Some people repeat the same reactions throughout their lives without stopping to realize that they are unconsciously imitating another person they have spent lots of time with. An example is the husband who frequently insults his wife because his dad frequently insulted *his* wife (the husband's mom). Other people "decide" at some point to act completely differently than a parent and take a 180 degree turn away from the one extreme only to unwittingly place themselves at the other. An example is the husband who never mentions his appropriate anger to his wife when she has truly offended him because he never wants to be like his dad. He buries his legitimate anger and wonders why his health suffers.

Acting Out: There's no place like home for letting it all hang out. Examples: children and teens throwing fits when they don't get what they want, adults losing their tempers and screaming at their kids, siblings tormenting each other, spouses loudly arguing hour after hour, day after day. There's no more "showy" way to demonstate that self-control is gone—which is weakness, not strength.

The kind of thinking that goes on during these acting out "demonstrations" is: "I sure told him!" "I've just had it. Now she knows she better not cross the line again!" "That little jerk will think twice before he says that to me one more time!" These kinds of thoughts are self-trickery because when we act out we do *not* win the respect of others nor genuine respect for ourselves. Down deep we know it.

Displacement: It happens to us all: we are at work, school, or some other place where someone, or some circumstance, makes us angry and we can't act out there. So when we get home we "take out our frustrations" on a child, spouse, sibling, or the cat--targets who can't fire us, give us a bad grade, or hurt us worse than we can hurt them. The angry person is like a booby trap. Any little irritation like a tricycle in the driveway will set him or her off. When the explosion happens, the exploding person actually thinks the upset is about the trike and the child needs to be "told" not to do it again, when in fact, the child who actually committed a minor offense is the hapless victim of a furious, overblown fit of temper that actually has nothing to do with the tricycle.

Scapegoating: Many families have a "black sheep" or at least one individual who almost always gets teased for any reason whatever and fingered for things that go wrong. In the beginning of this destructive pattern this individual usually *is* the one who manages to spill his or her milk at least once a day or say the wrong thing in front of company. But gradually, he or she starts taking the rap for every aggravating thing that happens in the family and becomes a consistent target for everyone's frustrations. In many cases the "scapegoat" settles into the black sheep role and forms the habit of annoying the other members of the family whenever possible. This can go on for decades and just get worse. Sometimes the results are tragic unless the pattern is broken.

Rivalries: Siblings are known for getting into conflicts and ongoing feuds. In some families the children appear by their behavior to hate each other intensely at times. These rivalries are so common that most people accept them as normal. But normal or not, the hurts caused by rivalries are only made worse when parents obviously favor certain children over others and compare them to one another. (Sometimes rivalries occur between family members other than siblings. Examples: spouses competing for greater levels of career success; a daughter and stepmother competing for the love and attention of the father and husband; cousins competing for the adoration of a grandparent.)

Take a L👀k at Your Own Family:

Which of these five types of actions (unconscious imitation, acting out, displacement, scapegoating, rivalries) are most likely to occur in your family?

_____

_____

_____

How does (or did) your mother handle her anger?

_____

_____

_____

How are (or were) you affected by it then and now?

_____

_____

_____

How does (or did) your father handle his anger?

_____

_____

_____

How are (or were) you affected by it then and now?

_____

_____

_____

Ideas for Stopping, and Re-Channeling, Destructive Behavior at Home

Start with yourself! People can manipulate and influence each other but no one can make another person act exactly the way he or she wants the other person to act. *The only individual each of us has control over is ourselves, if we will take that control!*

Go back over your list on the prior page of destructive actions that are most likely to happen in your family. Ask yourself how many of them you do yourself. This is making what was unconscious become conscious. It's a big challenge. Being honest with yourself in this way is the first step to improving the family dynamics in your home. Besides self-honesty this also takes courage, strength, *the right motive* and *consciousness!*

Unconscious Imitation: Do you ever find yourself automatically acting like someone (a family member or someone else) but you do not admire those actions? If yes, write some notes to yourself about how you unconsciously imitate another person's poor behavior at times with family members and how you could stop doing it.

_____

_____

_____

_____

Acting Out: Do you ever find yourself out of control, doing and saying things that you later realize were "over the top?" If yes, write some notes to yourself about how you act out at home at times and how you could stop doing it.

_____

_____

_____

_____

Displacement: Do you ever find yourself taking the frustrations you feel toward someone who has some sort of authority over you out on someone, or something, else? If yes, write some notes to yourself about how you displace your anger on a family member at times and how you could stop doing it.

_____

_____

_____

_____

Scapegoating: Do you ever find yourself frequently picking on someone in the family and/or assuming that person is the one at fault when something goes wrong? If yes, write some notes to yourself about how you scapegoat another family member at times and how you could stop doing it.

_____

_____

_____

_____

Rivalries: Do you find yourself competing and fighting with another member of your family at times? If yes, write some notes to yourself about how you engage in a rivalry with a family member and how you might end it.

_____

_____

_____

What if someone else in your family is being irrational and destructive?

Consider situations where it's obvious another person is not thinking sensibly and is behaving in hurtful ways toward you or someone else physically or psychologically. Situations and people are different, but let's come up with some ways to communicate with the person who's being destructive that could help:

Unconscious Imitation: What could you do, or not do, if someone is *unconsciously imitating* the destructive actions of someone else? Here are some ideas:

- It will *not* help to tell the person what you believe she is doing while she is doing it. For example, if you say, "You're acting the same hysterical way mom always acts when she's upset," the person will probably become even more upset.

- Don't play into the person's hands by acting the part of the other person in the original drama. For example: Dad used to blow up whenever something got broken and everyone else would cower. If his grown son unconsciously imitates Dad and does likewise, don't cower. Wait till he cools down. Then calmly discuss what happened.

- Show empathy. Try saying, "I'd be mad about that too. Let's figure out what to do."

- Do you have other ideas? List them here.

_____

_____

_____

_____

_____

Acting Out: What could you do, or not do, if someone is destructively *acting out* angry feelings? Here are some ideas:

- If the person is upset but does not seem dangerous, just listen with empathy. Say as little as possible. Let him "get it out of his system" until he is ready to talk sensibly. This may not be until the next day.

29

- If the person is raging and being destructive, or seems about to be destructive, don't try to reason with her because she won't hear a word you say. Don't get "suckered in" by the person who is spoiling for a fight or by anyone else who wants to see it happen. Keep eye contact, say nothing, or tell her you will discuss it with her later. Then slowly leave the scene.

- Do you have other ideas? List them here.

_____

_____

_____

_____

_____

_____

Displacement: What could you do, or not do, if someone is *taking out his anger* on another person in the family who is a weaker target than the actual cause of the anger? Here are some ideas:

- This is very similar to "acting out," (above). Since the angry person "thinks" he is justified in directing his anger at the weaker target, remove the target--you, or whoever else it might be. If it's someone else tell the angry person you will deal with it. Example: Mom was treated badly at work by her boss. She can't explode there but comes home loaded with animosity. Jimmy's tricycle is in the driveway when Mom drives up. She gets out of the car and furiously comes after Jimmy. Dad steps in and tells Mom he will handle it. He and Jimmy go outside and move the tricycle. They stay away from Mom until she has calmed down.

- If you are the intended victim, don't say anything; just get away from the angry person as soon as you can. Don't try to defend yourself with words. That just intensifies his outrage. Most important, do not allow yourself to be "dumped on." That's why you need to get away.

- Do you have other ideas? List them here.

_____

_____

_____

_____

Scapegoating: What could you do, or not do, if most, or all, of the members of your family *assume that one member is always to blame* when things go wrong? Here are some ideas:

- Do your part to change things in an obvious way. Make a conscious effort to give equal amounts of attention, appreciation and affection to *all* family members. Never tease anyone in the family unkindly.

- Turn things around for the scapegoat by complimenting him in front of everyone whenever possible for anything he might have done that you appreciate.

- When something goes wrong and the scapegoat is assumed to be guilty, suggest that blamers investigate and obtain proof before making accusations.

- If something goes wrong and it's not known who did it, question *everyone* who might have done it. If proof cannot be found that the scapegoat committed the offense, let it go.

- Cut the scapegoat the same slack everyone else gets.

- Do you have other ideas? List them here.

_____

_____

_____

_____

_____

_____

Rivalries: What could you do, or not do, if two or more people in the family are constantly *competing and sabotaging* each other? Here are some ideas:

- Find ways to get the rivals to be on the same team or work together to attain a goal that will benefit them both.

- Compliment and reward the rivals as equally as possible.

- Never, ever compare the rivals to each other, gossip about one to the other, or encourage them to have it out.

Do you have other ideas? List them here.

_____

_____

_____

_____

_____

_____

What does it take to use your anger constructively?

We've acknowledged that Honesty, Courage and Strength are the first steps in managing anger. People with these skills who others admire can admit their anger to themselves and are able to make a decision in full awareness to use the strong feeling they are having to get something done that needs to be done. Then these people don't chicken out. They push forward to do the constructive thing even if it's a long haul and they get little or no support.

The Right Motive!

Ask yourself: why do I want to do this? If it's "to hurt and get even" it is *not* constructive--it's destructive! It's extremely hard sometimes, but to manage anger well, you need to level with yourself and choose to use your anger to fuel actions that will benefit you and others, and not make anyone suffer.

Consciousness!

Have you noticed that all of the elements of anger management include being completely aware--*conscious*--of what you're feeling, thinking and doing? Being true to yourself is the bottom line--the necessary ingredient in any constructive action.

Let's look at some ways to stay conscious when angry:

Conscious Imitation: A few pages ago you looked at how easy it is to *unconsciously* imitate your parents and others. But imitation can also be conscious. Who do you know, or know of, who handles, or handled, their anger well? This is someone you can purposely try to act like.

Describe the way this individual has acted when angry that you can imitate *on purpose* when you feel the same way.

_____

_____

_____

_____

_____

_____

Conscious Self-Talk: When you think about situations, people, and your own reactions, you are "talking with yourself" whether you realize it or not. What kind of self-talk do you do? When angry do you work yourself up into more anger or do you face the feeling and then talk to yourself in ways that help? For example: here are some things you could say in your mind: "Chill out. Calm down. You can handle it. This will pass." (We will talk more about this strategy in Chapter Five.)

Write down at least one thought (a message you can purposely send to yourself) that can help you use your anger constructively:

_____

_____

_____

_____

_____

_____

Letting Off Steam Consciously: Sometimes each of us can get so mad that conscious anger management just can't happen and we know it. If you feel furious and the impulse to hurt someone, or yourself, is strong, that's when you can decide to let off some steam for awhile before trying to figure out what happened and what to do about it. Physical activities like running, hiking, lifting weights, dancing, gardening, or playing a sport, often work very well for people when they are stuck in an angry state. Others do it mentally: they concentrate on the words to a song or chant that calms them or they repeat words and phrases that settle themselves down (positive self-talk). Others just do something else for awhile that fully absorbs their attention until they feel better, like watching a movie, playing a musical instrument, or reading a book. (There will be more on this strategy, too, in Chapter Five.)

What works for you? Make a list.

_____

_____

_____

_____

_____

_____

HOMEWORK: Over the next few days go back over this chapter from time to time and fill in your responses to any questions you left blank. Reread sections that seemed difficult. These may be the ones you most need to learn.

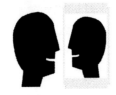

LIFE WORK: Over the next week pay close attention to anger and family dynamics in your home. Make your best effort not to do any of the destructive actions you have explored in this chapter and to help others to keep from doing them. Stay conscious throughout the week to your own motives and thoughts, especially when you are angry. Reflect often on your own actions.

Adelita is the name of a song about a beloved young woman who fought alongside the revolutionaries in Mexico during a series of battles in the first quarter of the 1900s. These battles occurred between poor mestizos--persons of mixed Indian and European blood--and one reigning government after another that oppressed them.

My mother-in-law was an Adelita, a fervent revolucionaria! Although her real name is different, the name Adelita suits her well for this true story so I will use it.

She was one of those heroines who wore gun belts across her chest and rode in boxcars across Mexico with the fighters. They were bonded to each other by their sense of purpose singing songs like La Cucaracha as they created mayhem on the establishment. To say they turned everything into chaos in the cities, towns and villages they invaded is an understatement. But, as in any war, things frequently got out of hand. Despite the noble intentions of the revolutionaries, the innocent frequently suffered along with the enemy, horrible cruelty often occurred, and confusion prevailed. Bands of fighters frequently fought each other for dominance and allegiances were betrayed. Bandits joined the fray and had a field day. To get the flavor of that time of camaraderie and death watch a movie like *Old Gringo* or read books like Mastretta's *Lovesick* and Michener's *Mexico*.

I didn't know any of this about my mother-in-law until she lay dying in a hospital in 1979 and by then it was too late to listen to her stories. A relative produced an old photo he'd found in a trunk and there was no mistake. It was her staring at the camera beside a young man. He wore gunbelts criss-crossed on his chest and a large sombrero. She was gripping a rifle and from her expression it was clear that she knew how to use it!

What a shock to all of us, her children, grandchildren and in-laws! Conversation sprang up immediately between us and we began to put two and two together. Prior to that time all we knew was that she had been born in a small Mexican town somewhere in the Sonoran desert named Ojo de Agua shortly after the turn of the century. As a child, she was allowed to go to school only through the third grade. She had been married twice, once to an older man by whom she bore twin girls before he died; one twin also died and one lived. The second marriage had been to a man her own age (the one in the photo?) who fathered her next child, another daughter. Later, Adelita travelled north to the United States with her mother and little girls and illegally entered Arizona where she met and married my husband's father a few years later. They had four children; my husband, Vicente, was the oldest. And that was all anyone knew!

Adelita didn't volunteer more information about her life before coming to the United States and rarely, if ever, did any of us ask for more. We thought we had the basic facts and generally understood that her earlier years had been rough. The subject of that time in her life was off-limits. Besides, she could be very difficult.

I met Vicente when we enrolled in a small college in southern California in 1956. We were still in our teens. After a few months of dating he took me to meet his family, the beginning of a very exciting and wonderful time in my life. I immediately became fond of his dad, sisters, and extended family. Unlike my family, they were dramatic people--expressive and full of life. They were also very friendly to me. Only Adelita remained reserved when I visited and said little in English which she spoke well enough, preferring her native tongue. (This motivated me to learn to speak Spanish, which I rapidly did.) She had a knack for keeping everyone off balance with strange remarks and she rarely smiled. When I asked Vicente if she liked me he surprised me by saying in convincing tones, "Oh yes, probably more than anyone else in the family."

As time went by I became accustomed to Adelita. We developed a mutual respect for one another but it was usually silent. It never occurred to me to find out who she was underneath her unreadable exterior. There were times of great fun when she participated. All of us, including Adelita laughed our insides out over a startling statement made by their parrot or mynah bird, and at hilarious jokes told in Spanish. Adelita was extremely generous and loyal to the members of the family. She always defended us when we got into scrapes even when it was our own fault just like a mother lion that cares for her own no matter what. Yet, like a lioness, Adelita stayed somewhat aloof even from those she loved.

Besides being somewhat removed, Adelita was often critical, agitated or fearful. She frequently embarrassed others by announcing some mistake they had made in front of everyone else. Often she verbally tormented her male grandchildren. At times she became anxiety stricken that immigration officers would come and deport her to Mexico. Sometimes she was heard at night sobbing or yelling what sounded like war cries in her sleep. I now realize that Adelita had serious mental and emotional problems that overtook her at times.

One experience I remember with a shudder brought out the worst in Adelita and, oddly, the best. Vicente and I were in our early thirties, had good jobs, and two

young sons, Ricardo who was two-years old and our little new-born, Daniel. The story begins on Valentine's Day, 1986.

Proud of our "upward mobility," Vicente and I had just purchased a brand new Lincoln Continental, a huge monster, and had taken his parents to brunch. Feeling magnanimous, Vicente told his mother that he would like to take her anyplace she wanted to go in the new car. Expecting her to ask for a day at Disneyland or a trip to the bullfights in Tijuana, we were surprised by her quick answer: a trip to her birthplace to visit her relatives with whom she corresponded but had not seen in decades.

To say the least, proper planning by anyone, especially Vicente and me, did not go into that trip. There were five adults, our little boys, and far too much luggage packed into our bright, shiny, *heavy* new car. Casually, Vicente asked his mother if she still knew the way to which she dismissively responded, "Claro, que si." (Of course!) So off we went.

The 600-mile trip east from California and then south to Hermosillo in Sonora began at dusk. It was long and uncomfortable, but that wasn't anything compared to what was coming. We had breakfast at dawn in Hermosillo and then Adelita directed us to the road that would take us to Ojo de Agua. With no hesitation, Vicente swung onto the little two-lane gravel road heading Northeast into the desert. Within a few miles the gravel vanished and we found ourselves on a heavily rutted, one-lane trail. And then it got worse!

Vicente and I spoke at once. "Where's the map?" I asked as he declared, "This can't be right!" But it was.

Just in front of us appeared a battered sign that we could barely read. It said,

MOCTEZUMA with an arrow pointing straight ahead. Adelita pointed to the sign and pronounced, "See, I told you. After we go through Moctezuma we come to Ojo de Agua." Her tone implied that it was very simple and no big deal. But by then I had found our road on the map and gaped at what I saw. The map showed that we were at least 100 miles south of Moctezuma and, not only that, Ojo de Agua wasn't even shown!

I handed the map to Vicente who looked at it and instantly stopped the car. He turned around to glare at his mother in the back seat. "Mama," he barked, "Didn't you realize how far we would have to drive on this terrible road in our brand new car?"

Astonishingly, Adelita replied, "I told you. Don't say I didn't tell you. I made sure you would know. Don't blame me. It's not my fault!"

"You never said a word about it, Mama," Vicente shot back, but this just invited more disclaimers.

"I *did* tell you," she shouted. "Don't act like I didn't. It's not my fault. It's all *your* fault."

That was just the beginning of the most painful trip I have ever taken. The ruts, rocks and brush in the trail got worse. At times the trail wasn't even visible. We had to ford three rivers which, *gracias a dios (thanks to God)*, were shallow and had firm bottoms. Several times everyone had to get out and carry luggage when we came to a river or a steep hill. The car was even charged by a bull who resented our presence in his territory. As bad as all this was we were also subjected to Adelita's repeated claims that she had warned us about the distance and the road conditions. She even criticized Vicente's driving!

Occasionally we passed travellers on foot or in old pickups and now and then we came to a village only to learn that it was not Moctezuma. But each time the people assured us that Moctezuma was very close when, in fact, it was still many miles away. Adelita kept up her unasked-for statements of nonresponsibility while we fumed. Once her husband told her to say no more but it didn't have any effect. I recall that this was one of the few times open hostilities clearly existed between Adelita, who was distressed by our annoyance with her, and the rest of us.

That evening we arrived at Ojo de Agua, a very small village of adobe homes with dirt floors and no electricity. It had no public buildings and was surrounded by crops and grazing fields. The family there was expecting us and rejoiced at our arrival. Although we were exhausted and upset this warm welcome by such friendly souls abruptly changed our mood. As we brought our luggage into the little house and were shown our cots, a dozen neighborhood children came in to stare at the strangers, particularly me--a gringita!

One of the biggest surprises was Adelita's transformation. As if waking from a nap she cheerfully made all the introductions and remained absolutely charming throughout the four-day visit. However, she predictably became transformed back into the same person who rode with us from Hermosillo as soon as we pulled away for the trip home in our scratched and dirty automobile.

The trip north to the Arizona border was a mere 60 miles and we only had one river to ford, but the road was just as bad, maybe worse. About every fifteen minutes Adelita would break the strained silence with, "Don't blame me. I told you. Don't say I didn't."

Years later as she lay in the hospital and the family looked at that amazing photograph thoughts were shared about Adelita's past and how her experiences had affected her. One person mentioned that she'd been told her twin girls were born prematurely at a bad time. All she had was a shoebox to place them in. No wonder one died. Another said he'd heard how one of her husbands had been active in the revolution and was shot by a government firing squad.

The revolutionaries preferred "to die on their feet than live on their knees" as Emiliano Zapata put it. But war is a terrible business. As a teenager participating in the revolution, what did Adelita see? What did she do, or participate in doing? What did she personally suffer and what demons haunted her that never went away? Perhaps it was on the road to Ojo de Agua that horrible things happened.

Today I find myself wondering what my life would have been like if I'd been part of that turmoil. I also find myself wishing that I could be in Adelita's presence once again so we could talk as we never talked before. I would open my mind and forget the idea that she was a difficult person. If she were willing to tell me about herself and her experiences I would listen.

Chapter Three:
Anger and Interpersonal Communication

You have probably noticed how some people are able to talk with other people and make friends so easily that it seems they were born with these abilities. And have you noticed that other people seem to have the opposite nature: communication and friendships come hard for them? Perhaps you've noticed your own good days and days that aren't so good when it comes to interacting with others.

What's going on? To some extent the ability to develop "people skills" are no doubt woven into our genes, but the main way we develop them, or not, has to do with *learning* followed by the *formation of habits.* Lucky people grow up around others who know how to communicate skillfully and create good friendships. The vast majority of people, however, have not been around great models of interpersonal communication most of their lives and have not had a chance to take a class on the subject either. Yet, everyone can benefit from gaining information and tips on how to communicate well because all of us find ourselves with other people almost constantly and are likely to have developed some unhelpful habits that we aren't even aware we've got. Not only that, no one has become perfect at relationships. Even the best of the best can get better, and they are frequently the ones who seek to improve their skills and gain additional ones.

Why be concerned about interpersonal communication skills?

The fact is that most people who are terminated from their jobs don't get fired because they couldn't do the job. Rather, they are dismissed because they lack the ability to get along with customers, co-workers, or bosses. Most marriages don't end in divorce because husbands and wives didn't love each other when they got married or because they don't know how to run a household. The marriages end because these couples communicated poorly with each other, or failed to communicate at all. Most children who stay away from their parents as much as they can don't stay away because they don't love their parents. They create distance because communication with their parents is often frustrating or painful. The fact is that these kinds of problems can be avoided when people's hearts are in the right place and when they have *learned* how to communicate without causing hassles.

Why create hassles and rub people the wrong way when you don't have to? This chapter focuses on what skilled communicators do, and don't do, to build strong, positive relationships with others. These, in turn, *prevent* angry flare-ups and unnecessary, destructive conflicts.

Your Body Speaks Your Truth

In the last chapter we talked about anger and family dynamics. Your Life Work assignment was to watch the ways the members of your family deal with their anger. As you watched, did you notice how their bodies "spoke?" In fact, right now, if you are around people, or even a television that's turned on, stop and observe how people's bodies communicate their feelings, moods, motives, and even what they might be thinking. In fact, "body language," also known as "non-verbal communication," generally speaks louder than words.

Did you know that every time you communicate with others your body sends signals that cause people to decide whether or not you are someone they can respect, whether or not they want to remain in your company, and whether or not to believe and trust you. Usually without realizing it, people rely more on the messages they receive from your body language than from your spoken language. Also, you may not be aware that *you* are communicating some non-verbal messages you don't really want to send. Unhelpful non-verbal habits are easy to form. Becoming aware of them is the first step to dropping them and replacing them with useful habits.

Let's take a look at the ways your body speaks using these combined non-verbal signals:

Eye contact
Facial expressions
Gestures
Posture
Positioning and movement

Each one of these forms of non-verbal communication is important so let's talk about them one by one.

40

Eye contact

Have you ever been in a conversation with someone who hardly looked at you or didn't look at you at all? How did the person's lack of eye contact cause you to feel?

_____

_____

_____

_____

_____

_____

In some cultures prolonged eye-contact is considered rude. However, in western culture the opposite is true. Withholding eye contact from someone usually sends a negative message including contempt, disgust, or boredom. (Sometimes shyness causes lack of eye contact.) It's hard to tell why someone is withholding eye contact, but when it happens, it usually creates a barrier between the individuals.

At times this barrier occurs when a listener actually hears the message of a speaker more clearly when looking away, taking notes, or doodling, than when looking at the speaker. This is true for people who hear and learn best in the auditory mode. That is, through their ears. If this is true for you, let the main people in your life know it so they won't draw a negative conclusion when you look away from them while they are talking with you. It would also help to train yourself to establish some eye contact with others to let them know *for sure* that you *are* listening.

Blinking is a form of "interrupted" eye-contact. Natural blinking is no problem, but when a person blinks more than the normal amount during a conversation it usually signals a sign of weakness: perhaps anxiety or shyness.

Facial Expressions

When you are "being yourself" your face registers your changing feelings, thoughts, and moods. Unless you decide to put on an act to give a false impression, other people can usually "read you like a book." It's amazing to see the impact a smile or frown has on people who are looking at you. You can say almost anything but the way your statement will register on listeners relates as much to the expression on your face as it will to the statement itself, maybe more. When combined, your facial expressions and eye contact, or lack of it, send "loud and clear signals" to others about your attitudes toward them.

Recall the expressions on the face of someone you recently talked with. What message did those expressions send you and how did they make you feel?

_____

_____

_____

_____

_____

_____

Gestures

Have you focused on what people's bodies were doing when they were talking with each other and you couldn't hear what they were saying? Perhaps some people were speaking with each other at a distance or maybe you were watching a soap opera with the sound turned off. It's amazing how much you can tell about conversations and relationships just by watching peoples' gestures. Arms, hands, shoulders, head; even legs and feet actively emphasize spoken words. Combined with whether or not people are making eye contact with each other and their facial expressions, gestures send powerful non-verbal messages.

Watch someone who is nearby, whether they are speaking with you or someone else. Describe the gestures you see them use and state what you think the gestures are saying.

_____

_____

_____

_____

_____

_____

POSTURE

Like gestures, your posture speaks along with your spoken language. The way you stand, sit, and "hold yourself" says a lot about you, particularly how you feel about yourself. People who stand tall, or sit straight when seated, communicate a sense of dignity and self-possession to others. Their poise commands respect and what they have to say is much more likely to be taken seriously than the statements of people who hunch over and let their bodies sag. Likewise, when people with good posture listen to others it seems more obvious that they are listening carefully and respectfully than listeners with poor posture who are likely to seem less interested.

Think of someone you know whom you respect and enjoy talking with. Describe the person's usual posture.

_____

_____

_____

_____

_____

_____

POSITIONING AND MOVEMENT

When you are with other people do you face them while communicating, or do you turn your body from them, or even move away? Do you remain calm and still or do you pace, kick your foot out repeatedly, bite your fingernails, or move about in some other manner? Facing and looking straight at people you are communicating with while remaining still are ways to send non-verbal messages of sincerity and integrity. This puts others at ease and generally makes conversations worthwhile. Turning away, walking away, and moving about, distract the people you are communicating with and make them wonder what your problem might be.

Ask yourself who makes you nervous when you try to communicate with him or her because of strange positioning and movements. Describe how the person acts and how you feel about it.

_____

_____

_____

_____

_____

_____

43

WHAT ABOUT "YOUR" BODY LANGUAGE?

Go back to the list of the five main types of body language on page 40. Circle the ones you would like to improve. Then write some notes to yourself here about habits you may have formed that you wish to drop and how you can strengthen others that are desirable.

_____

_____

_____

_____

_____

_____

What About Your Spoken Language?

Some people have a gift for speaking. Others have developed the habit of not speaking enough and leave their friends and family wondering what they are thinking and feeling. Many people complain that the important people in their lives don't communicate with them. What about you? Do you share your thoughts and feelings with others, or do you withhold them? Admit it to yourself if you need to speak your truth more often. *Or perhaps less.*

When speaking are you clear, direct, and concise, or do you confuse and frustrate your listeners with vague, rambling, repetitive, and overly wordy statements? Is your tone generally calm and pleasant with appropriate inflection in your voice, or do you speak in a frenzied, irritating voice with too much emphasis? Perhaps you don't speak loudly and forcefully enough with little inflection so that people have to strain to listen and have to make an effort to be interested in what you have to say. Admit it to yourself if you have developed some unhelpful speaking habits and need to improve your speaking style.

What kind of feedback do you usually receive from others about the way you speak?

_____

_____

_____

_____

Do you wish to improve your ability to speak? In what ways?

_____

_____

_____

_____

_____

_____

Good Communicators are Good Listeners!

Almost everyone agrees that the most powerful and effective communication skill is listening! Good listeners are those people who let speakers know they care about them and are hearing every word. They do this by saying little, or not speaking at all. Sometimes they ask pertinent questions and grunt at appropriate times. They also let speakers know they are listening by using their non-verbal skills: solid eye-contact, open facial expression, gestures that say, "I'm interested," and straightforward body posture. They also position themselves facing the speaker with no distracting movements.

Name some people you like to talk with because they are good listeners. Describe their listening habits.

_____

_____

_____

_____

_____

_____

The Communication Stoppers!

The art of good conversation is not so much saying the right thing at the right time but not saying the wrong thing at the tempting moment! Do you know anyone who is difficult and unpleasant to communicate with? Chances are they have developed some poor habits they aren't even aware of, which have the effect of stopping communication. All of these actions tell others, "I have my own agenda and I'm not interested in listening to what you have to say."

Here's a list of eight of the most common Communication Stoppers:

Interrupting　　**Probing**　　**Dominating**　　**Judging**

Giving Unasked-for Advice　　**Misinterpreting**

Accusing / Criticizing　　**Putting down / Name calling**

Even the best communicators act in these ways from time to time. The purpose of looking at the communication stoppers is not to make you feel guilty. Rather, it is to help you become aware of things you might do that block communication and hurt your relationships. Awareness then allows you to become more in charge of yourself.

Interrupting

Interrupting is probably the most common and easiest communication stopper to use. It is simply butting in while someone else is speaking.

How do you feel when people interrupt you when you would rather have them listen?

_____

_____

_____

Probing

Asking questions in conversations is normal and even useful to increase understanding. But have you ever tried to tell someone something and they repeatedly shot question after question at you to get information that didn't fit into your story and didn't matter to you. That's probing. It includes interrupting because probers interrupt speakers as they bombard them with their questions.

How do you feel when people probe you in a conversation when you would rather have them listen?

_____

_____

_____

Dominating

Some people are on transmit 98% of the time, or close to it. They have developed the habit of taking over conversations and seem completely unaware that you might like to say something too. First they interrupt, then the avalanche of words comes next.

How do you feel when people dominate you in a conversation when you would rather have them listen?

_____

_____

_____

Judging

Judgmental people seem to feel called upon to make ratings; they rate you, other people, anything at all. They often apply labels: "good," "bad," "adequate," "inadequate," etc. It's natural, and even necessary, to form opinions. However, judging someone to his, or her, face--even when it's a positive judgement--can put a damper on the conversation because judging creates a feeling of inequality. It's like saying, "I'm superior to you; I'm the judge."

How do you feel when people judge you when you would rather have them listen with an open mind?

_____

_____

_____

Giving Unasked-for Advice

Some people just can't listen with empathy and understanding when you talk about a problem; they prefer to tell you how to solve it. They think they are being helpful but fail to realize that perhaps you just want to be listened to. When given unasked-for advice people often feel unheard and talked-down to.

How do you feel when people give you advice you didn't ask for when you would rather have them listen?

_____

_____

_____

Misinterpreting

Some people just can't seem to listen long enough and well enough to get your message straight. They jump to conclusions and make incorrect assumptions about what you are saying and twist your words to mean something you didn't mean at all. Often when you try to correct their interpretation things get worse.

How do you feel when people misinterpret your words when you would rather have them listen more carefully?

_____

_____

_____

Accusing / Criticizing

Some people give in to the urge to blame and criticize when they are disappointed or angry with another person before hearing his or her side of the story. Even when someone has done something wrong, accusations and criticism will probably not lead to a helpful conversation about the cause of the wrong action or how to correct it.

How do you feel when people who believe you have done something wrong accuse and criticize you without listening to what you have to say?

_____

_____

_____

Putting down / Name calling

Even when joking around, put-downs and unflattering labels can hurt. When said with the intention to hurt they can hurt very much, indeed. Some people put others down and call them names because *they* are frequently put down and called names themselves. They seem to feel that the bad feelings should be shared and spread around. Whatever the reason for behaving like this, they do not build friendships and consistently drive people away.

How do you feel when people put you down or call you names?

_____

_____

_____

Be Straight with Yourself!

Go back to page 46 and draw a circle around the communication stoppers you know you do to others too often. Write yourself a few notes about who you wish to listen to better in the future and which "stoppers" you intend to stop using with them.

_____

_____

_____

_____

_____

_____

_____

_____

Take some credit!

Can you remember a time you held your tongue when you felt like saying something that probably would have spoiled, or stopped, communication with someone? Describe it here:

_____

_____

_____

_____

_____

_____

_____

_____

_____

_____

The Highest Level of Listening

Can you remember a time when you listened to someone's feelings with "your third ear" in order to demonstrate feelings of caring and compassion? Perhaps the person was being obnoxious, boastful or completely unreasonable. Or maybe the person was wrong about something but insisting that he or she was right. At times like this it can be very difficult to respond to the person's real emotions which are hidden beneath the surface because for most people the urge to be harsh with the person is strong. Frequently, when people are being the most annoying that's when they are probably most in need of kind understanding. Down deep they may be feeling unappreciated, hurt, insecure, fearful, forgotten about, discounted, and anxious when they are bothering you with disagreeable behavior.

When this happens it could be a good time to try listening with your third ear—sort of like "reading between the lines." (If the person is dumping on you, however, it's a different situation. Do not accept abuse.)

Here's the process for listening with your third ear:

1. Acknowledge your own feeling about the person's behavior. (This may be someone you like, or even love, but at the moment they are not behaving attractively.)

2. Acknowledge what you feel like saying to the person and decide not to say it.

3. Determine the person's inner feelings.

4. If you determine that the person is feeling unappreciated, hurt, insecure, fearful, forgotten about, discounted, or anxious, say something reassuring to him, or her, to reduce the uncomfortable feelings.

This takes patience and effort, but there are two rewards: the person usually stops the annoying behavior, and you will no doubt gain a strong surge of positive personal power!

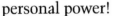

Give "Listening with Your Third Ear" a try. Here are two exercises to challenge you to practice this highest level of listening.

George and Gail

George and Gail are brother and sister. They are both in their early twenties and care for each other. But George and Gail have frequently argued and fought with each other during their entire lives. These disagreements have usually been over unimportant matters with Gail contradicting her brother far more often than he has contradicted her. Their parents have often said, "What does it matter?" but the debates continued. During a recent visit to their parent's home Gail started one argument after another with George. Finally, she insisted that a friend of theirs went to Lincoln High School after George stated that he went to Jackson High. George is correct and knows she's wrong.

If you were George how would you feel about Gail's behavior?

_____

_____

_____

What would you *feel* like saying to her?

_____

_____

_____

Why is Gail acting this way? How is she probably feeling inside?

_____

_____

_____

What could George say to Gail to reduce her uncomfortable feelings and encourage her to be less disagreeable?

_____

_____

_____

_____

Jamie and his mom

Jamie is in the third grade. One day he became so difficult in class that his teacher called his mom to tell her about it. Jamie's mom listened and agreed that kicking other children and yelling, "I hate school!" during class was completely unacceptable. "Yes," said the teacher. "We were having awards and just because he didn't get one he got mad." When Jamie came home he slammed the door and threw his books and papers down on the kitchen floor. His mom asked for an apology and made him pick up the mess. She told Jamie about the call from his teacher and told him she was very disappointed in his behavior. That night at dinner Jamie's dad brought home an early birthday present for Jamie's little brother who wasn't celebrating his birthday for two more weeks. That did it. Jamie pounded on the table. Then he ran to his room. His mom waited for about 10 minutes. Then she followed him there.

If you were Jamie's mom how would you feel about his behavior?

_____

_____

_____

What would you *feel* like saying to him?

_____

_____

_____

Why is Jamie acting this way? How is he probably feeling inside?

_____

_____

_____

What could Jamie's mom say to him to reduce his uncomfortable feelings and encourage him to be less disagreeable?

_____

_____

_____

_____

Understanding and Reassurance

Describe a time when you listened to someone's real feelings and responded in an understanding and reassuring way. If you can't remember doing this, life will probably give you an opportunity soon. After it happens write about it here.

_____

_____

_____

_____

_____

_____

How does listening with your third ear make you feel about yourself?

_____

_____

_____

_____

_____

HOMEWORK: Go back through this chapter and reread the parts that were the most challenging for you. If you left any questions unanswered, fill in your responses. Over the next few months reread this chapter again and write updated answers to the questions, perhaps in ink of a different color. You will likely notice that your responses reflect interesting changes in your thoughts and attitudes.

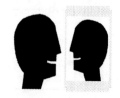

LIFE WORK: Make it a point to observe other people and yourself in non-verbal and verbal communication situations. See how often you can "plug in" helpful body language and stop yourself from using "communication stoppers." Remember to "listen with your third ear" when you become aware that it might be the best thing to do for someone.

Life lessons can be vividly learned from our own experiences and the experiences of others told as stories. Tales, fables, and legends are also great teachers.

One of my favorite old tales is about a Native American boy and his grandfather. No one seems to know who wrote this story or where it comes from, but it's a good one. The boy in the story was angry and resentful because a friend had done him an injustice. He went to his old grandfather and told him about it.

The boy's grandfather said, "I, too, have felt great anger and hate toward people who have taken so much and not been ashamed of their actions. But feelings like that only hurt *you*, not your enemy. It's like taking poison and wishing your enemy would die. I have struggled with these kinds of feelings many times. It is as if there are two wolves inside me. One is good and never harms anyone. He lives in harmony with his surroundings and does not become offended when no offense was intended. He only fights when he has to and he does it fairly.

"But the other wolf...ah!" the grandfather continued, "the littlest thing sends him into a fury. He is disagreeable and fights others for no reason. He can't think straight because his anger and hate cloud his mind. His anger-driven behavior is useless because it only makes things worse. It is difficult to live sometimes with these two wolves inside me, for each one wants to control my spirit."

The boy looked intently into his grandfather's eyes and asked, "Grandfather, which one wins?"

The grandfather smiled and quietly said, "The one I feed."

I wish I'd heard and understood this story as a child so I could have learned much earlier how futile and corrosive it is to hold a grudge and indulge in feuding. At various points in my earlier life I threw myself into ongoing "wars" with individuals who annoyed me as much as I apparently bothered them. I recall that the first such war began on my first day in the first grade. That's when I met my nemesis, Paulie Barkoware, with whom I did battle for six years until we finally went to separate junior high schools.

I didn't hit it off so well with the teacher that day either. She called the roll, then asked, "Is there anyone here who's name I did not call?" I raised my hand.

"What is your name, dear?" she asked and I responded, "Gerry Dunne."

"I did call your name, dear," the teacher said rather sharply. "Here it is right here: Geraldine Dunne."

"That's not my name."

"Yes, it is," the teacher retorted. "Don't you know your own name?"

"My name is Gerry," I said as the children howled with laughter and my face turned red. Paulie seemed to be the one most delighted with my embarrassment. His loud laughter sounded like a braying mule.

"Gerry is your nickname, dear," the teacher patiently explained when the laughter subsided. "Your name is Geraldine. I'm surprised you don't know that." Then her face lit up. "That reminds me," she announced. "We have a book about Geraldine!"

She got up and went to the bookshelf and brought back a whole stack of booklets.

Lifting the top one to show us the cover, the teacher chirped, "Here it is. It's one of our readers, *Geraldine, The Cow!*"

Even now I remember the humiliation I felt in the moments that followed. The hoots of my peers, especially Paulie's, were deafening and I wanted to strangle him or die on the spot. For the rest of that day, and every single day after that through the sixth grade, Paulie tormented me with cow remarks. All he had to do was moo at me and laugh to send me into a fit of temper. Since his laughter reminded me of a donkey I made braying noises at him.

This sounds like the silly play of little kids, doesn't it? But as far as I was concerned it was very serious and deadly indeed. At times I became so upset when Paulie razzed me that I slapped or kicked him, which earned me a referral to the principal's office whenever I got caught.

"Why did you kick your classmate?" The principal would typically ask.

"Cuz he called me a name," I would typically answer.

"Shame on you, Geraldine," he would typically respond. "Always remember: sticks and stones can break your bones, but names will never hurt you."

How wrong and confusing that statement seemed. How unfair I thought it was that Paulie wasn't the one in trouble when *he* started it. How trapped I felt in a situation I didn't know how to change.

Over the years those very same feelings of mounting resentment and frustration occurred again from time to time during my life as a result of other wars I waged with various individuals at home, school and work. Emotionally, I was that five-year old hearing Paulie bray when the teacher cheerfully showed us that horrible book or being shamed by the principal and listening to his standard lecture which made no sense to me. And just as I did as a child, I reacted by lashing out from time to time when provoked and found myself the loser. Sound familiar?

One of the few really good things about becoming older for people like me who take time to "get it" is having the opportunity to look back and finally figure things out. Just like the Native American boy's grandfather who explained that he still struggles with the two wolves inside him, I still struggle at times with difficult people and situations. Doesn't everybody?

I have reached some conclusions, however, that serve me as guidelines for self possession and control when I feel myself becoming that hurt and angry five-year old again. Let me share them with you:

For years I didn't want to be a scrapper anymore. I thought the way to avoid hurt and "unpleasantness" was to repress my feelings and deny painful experiences. Then something would happen to cause the volcano inside me to explode and no one would be more surprised than me. I also made myself very sick and almost died twice because I swallowed so much "poison." Now I understand that feelings are indicators like signs on the road. It's up to me to decide what to do with the information those feelings give me just like I would decide where to drive my car after reading the signs.

I learned not to make assumptions. Jumping to conclusions is risky and can lead to terrible consequences. Nothing taught me this more clearly than meeting Paulie Barkoware again one night when we were in our thirties. He recognized me at a party and approached saying, "Moo, Geraldine!" I almost spilled my plate of food. "Weren't we crazy kids?" he asked, and without waiting for an answer because I was speechless, said, "You know, Gerry, when that whole cow thing started I was just trying to get you to pay attention to me because I thought you were cute. I wasn't very good at making friends with girls." After I found my voice Paulie and I laughed and talked for awhile. It was one of the most healing and enlightening experiences of my life and made me realize how I had simply *assumed* that Paulie detested me so I detested *him*. Now I try to make it a habit to ask questions in puzzling situations and get evidence before I reach conclusions.

I realized that I shouldn't take so many things personally. Occasionally someone's action, or lack of action, is clearly offensive and designed to hurt me, but not very often. Even then, what other people do is not about me, it's about *them*! People do what they do because of their own "programs," which in some cases can be very unhealthy. Their burdens belong to them and mine belong to me. This view keeps me free of being a victim.

It was hard, but I finally learned to let go of grudges. Revenge is sweet for a very short time. After getting back at someone things almost always turn sour again right away. When someone offends me I don't have to offend them in return or accept it lying down either. There's a middle course I can take if I want to be smart. This course offers strategies I can use to handle the offender and hold on to myself at the same time.

And last, I decided to feed only the good wolf! I try my best to send the bad one into the woods with his tail between his legs!

Chapter Four:
Anger and Conflict Management Strategies

Did you know that the main ways people operate with each other could be placed in three categories? These ways are often referred to as "styles" and tend to show up clearly in us all when tense situations occur. They include our attitudes, or mind state (self-talk), and the actions we engage in. The three styles are known as (1) the aggressive style (which, in this case, has nothing to do with being a successful business go-getter), (2) the submissive style, and (3) the assertive style. Only the assertive style includes *managing* anger and conflict. The other two usually allow anger in conflict situations to lead to destructive outcomes.

All of the strategies for managing anger and conflict described in this chapter and Chapter Five are assertive strategies; they are part and parcel of the assertive style. Before we look at the strategies, however, let's find out more about the three styles.

The Aggressive Style:

People who are aggressive with other people have a "me first" attitude. Many aggressive people are seen as pushy, hotheads or bullies. Others can appear to be sensitive and even charming but in truth are not concerned with anyone's well being but their own. Aggressive people are known for not playing fair. They will take advantage of others whenever they get the chance. They frequently try to intimidate and overpower others with subtle or clearly stated threats. Sometimes they are hostile and use harsh words as well as other forms of verbal violence. Sometimes they become physically violent.

What is the mind state (self-talk) of aggressive people? Their thoughts are:

- "My way or the highway."
- "Get them before they get you."
- "The best defense is an offense."
- "How you play doesn't count, only that you win."
- "Never give a sucker an even break."
- "Don't bother thinking or talking things over; just do what you have to do."

How do aggressive people act?

- These people intentionally attack, take advantage of, humiliate, hurt, and put other people down.
- They are usually outraged if anyone treats them the same way.
- Sometimes they act covertly like gossiping, or starting ugly rumors.
- If someone behaves offensively toward them they immediately counterattack.
- They jump to conclusions and react to situations based on assumptions that are often not correct.
- They surround themselves with people they can easily control.

Do you know someone who frequently thinks and acts in the aggressive style? How do you feel about him, or her?

_____

_____

_____

Note: Many people who act aggressively have been hurt by other aggressive people and actually feel weak and insecure inside. They behave aggressively as a false protective shield and don't want anyone to know how they really feel about themselves.

The Submissive Style:

Submissive people generally feel insecure and frequently show it. They are often afraid to stand up for themselves and frequently allow other people take advantage of them. Submissive people are known to put themselves down, apologize when they should be the one apologized to, and constantly seek the approval of others.

What is the mind state (self-talk) of submissive people? Their thoughts are:

- "I always get things wrong."
- "Other people are more important than me."
- "I must never cause anyone to be disappointed or disapprove of me."
- "I should never say no to anyone for any reason."
- "I should never give anyone a stomach ache or headache except myself."
- "I don't have the right to ask questions about situations I don't understand."

How do submissive people act?

- Submissive people permit others to hurt, humiliate, or take advantage of them.
- They frequently grovel and make negative statements about themselves.
- If someone behaves offensively toward them, they immediately give in and give way.
- They rarely speak up with their opinion, or ask questions about situations they don't understand.
- They allow themselves to be chosen as companions by people who easily control them.

Do you know someone who frequently thinks and acts in the submissive style? How do you feel about him, or her?

_____

_____

_____

THE ASSERTIVE STYLE:

Assertive people don't resort to the tactics of aggressive people, but they are not wimps! They stand up for themselves while remaining cool and calm. They are respectful, but direct, about their feelings, needs, and desires. They are confident and they know their rights. However, *they know and respect the rights of others as well.*

What is the mind state (self-talk) of assertive people? Their thoughts are:

- "I know that all individuals are equally important, including me."
- "I know how I feel, what I need, and what I want. I can state my feelings, needs and wants to other people when I choose to."
- "I have the right for ask for what I want, or need, and other people have the right to say yes, or no. I can't complain if I don't get what I wanted, but didn't ask for it."
- "Other people have an equal right to ask for what they want, or need. And I have the right to say yes, or no."
- "If I don't understand a situation I can ask questions to find out what I need to know."

How do assertive people act?

- Assertive people express themselves openly and honestly to communicate their feelings, wants, and needs without demanding them. They show respect for the feelings, wants and needs of others. They understand that each individual has a point of view.
- If someone's behavior toward them is offensive they ask what the problem is without attacking back or becoming defensive.
- When they don't understand what's going on they ask questions.
- They select companions who are also assertive.

Do you know someone who frequently thinks and acts in the assertive style? How do you feel about him, or her?

_____

_____

_____

_____

_____

Identify them:

Try this exercise. For each of the following situations write in the words "Aggressive," "Submissive," or "Assertive" next to the description of a mind state (self-talk) or a behavior of each type:

Mark and Hank:

On the way from the parking lot to the office Mark approaches his co-worker, Hank, and says: "Quick. Let me see your report." Hank asks why and Mark says, "So I can get some ideas from it. Quit stalling."

Hank's thoughts before he does anything are:

_____ "I did the work and he didn't. It's not fair for him to take advantage of me like this. I'm going to tell him so."

_____ "I better give it to him because he'll get mad and start calling me names if I don't."

_____ "What nerve! I'm going to tell him what an useless jerk he is."

60

Marlene and James:

Marlene is a high school student. One morning her parents asked her to baby-sit her younger brother, James, that afternoon. Marlene agreed and came home as soon as she could and waited for James to come home too. (He attended the afternoon kindergarten class at a nearby elementary school.) She waited and waited but there was no sign of James who went to a friend's house and forgot all about coming home. Marlene was so worried about James she became frantic. She called the homes of several of his friends but no one knew where he was. Finally, two hours later, James walked in through the front door. The minute Marlene saw him she said:

"You miserable, inconsiderate little brat! Where on earth have you been? I'm gonna teach you a lesson you'll never forget!"

"James! Thank goodness you're here. I didn't know *what* to do. Please don't tell Mom and Dad that I couldn't find you."

"James, I've been waiting two hours for you to come home. I've been extremely worried about you and I'm very upset. Where have you been and what have you been doing?"

Angela, Randy and Nancy:

Angela's family has recently moved into the neighborhood so she's "the new girl" at the high school. She wants to make friends so whenever she can she smiles at the other students and says "Hi." When she greets Randy he stops to talk with her in a friendly way. Later Randy's girlfriend, Nancy, approaches Angela. Nancy says:

"Hi. I'm Nancy. I've noticed how friendly you are. In fact, I saw you talking with my boyfriend, Randy, a few minutes ago. Where did you move here from?"

"Gee, you're cute, Angela. Randy will probably want you to be his girlfriend instead of me."

"Hey you, whatever your name is! Just keep your grubby hands off Randy. He's mine!"

Brian and Rob:

Brian Harris teaches five science classes and one math class. Each class has about thirty-five students, which means he has over 200 students' names to learn at the beginning of each semester. One day during the first week of class he calls a student "Bob," whose name is actually Rob. Rob reacts in an insulting manner saying, "Can't anyone get my name right? It's Rob, old man." Before responding Brian Harris thinks to himself:

"What a twerp! I'll put him in his place soon enough."
"What's wrong with me? I did it again. I wish I could remember names better."
"I don't like his attitude but I understand his feelings. That probably happens to him a lot."

How assertive are *you*?

The next time you find yourself in a provoking situation stop to notice your thoughts and actions. Are they aggressive, submissive, or assertive? Even if they are assertive you can probably improve in developing a *consistent* assertive style. This is true for almost everyone because few people are able to be assertive 100% of the time in all situations.

Assertive people manage themselves first! Their self respect and self control shows in the way they act. Both their body language and spoken language are open and straightforward. Their tone of voice is calm and even. They are aware of how important it is to act respectfully toward others and to "talk to themselves" in helpful ways when they become stressed.

Assertive people would point out that the most important person you are in contact with every day is yourself. You live with your self-talk--messages you constantly send to yourself.

When you listen in on your thoughts, what do you hear? Every day you are at the mercy of hundreds of influences like other people, the media, and your own impulses. Without helpful self-talk it's very difficult for people to manage themselves and stay away from places they don't really want to go, especially when they become angry.

Ghandi, a man who had the personal power to change history, put it this way:

Keep your thoughts positive because your thoughts become your words.
Keep your words positive because your words become your behaviors.
Keep your behaviors positive because your behaviors become your habits.
Keep your habits positive because your habits become your values.
Keep your values positive because your values become your destiny.

Think of a recent time when you used positive self-talk to help yourself. Jot down what you said to yourself and how it helped you here:

_____

_____

_____

_____

_____

_____

_____

_____

_____

_____

_____

Conflict Happens!

Because we live in a world populated with other people with their own needs and points of view, conflict is inevitable and normal just like anger. And just like anger, conflict can result in constructive or destructive outcomes. The diagram on the next page shows three different types of outcomes from conflict whether they occur between nations, groups, members of families, or two individuals.

The third outcome in the diagram shows that when everyone involved in a conflict sincerely desires a fair outcome and thinks and acts assertively no one has to get hurt. Sometimes conditions can even be *improved* because the conflict happened. This occurs when the people involved consciously manage their anger and use conflict management strategies. (There is no guarantee that whenever you find yourself in a conflict the other people involved will sincerely desire a fair outcome and think and act assertively too. But if *you* behave assertively instead of falling into aggressive or submissive behavior you stand a good chance of influencing the others involved to behave assertively as well.)

Three Types of Conflict

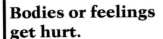

Bodies or feelings get hurt. 	One person gets hurt and the other gets his, or her, way. 	No one gets hurt.
What happens: Both parties attack each other. Verbal violence (and possibly physical violence) occurs.	**What happens:** One party attacks and overpowers the other using verbal violence (and possibly physical violence).	**What happens:** No one attacks anyone else in a verbal or physical way. Each person speaks for himself, or herself. Each person listens to the other. Both parties agree on a way to settle the conflict.
Results: Things are worse than they were at first. Both parties disrespect each other. Both parties disrespect themselves.	**Results:** The conflict may seem to be settled... BUT both parties disrespect each other. Both parties disrespect themselves even if the "victor" won't admit it.	**Results:** The conflict gets settled. Both parties respect each other. Both parties respect themselves.

Let's take a look at some conflict management strategies.

I Messages!

Why is it that some people have lots of friends and rarely get into fights with anyone? It isn't because they never become provoked. Sometimes they do find themselves in conflicts and when it happens they usually have a way of settling things easily and quickly with the other person so they can remain on good terms with each other. These people aren't magic--they just have an assertive skill which gives them power. This skill is the ability to use "I Messages."

Imagine that you are in a class and have come late several times. Now the teacher is talking with you about it. Read what the teacher says and then write your reaction.

"You failed to turn up on time again--probably because you didn't care enough to get ready and leave on time so you could get here when class started. You'd better watch that tardiness habit and stop being so flakey."

How did the teacher's remarks make you feel?

_____

_____

_____

_____

Now, let's do a replay. The teacher is speaking with you about the same thing but in a different way:

"I'm feeling concerned that you weren't here again when we began class today because you miss things. I regret it because you don't get to hear the opening remarks, which set the tone for the session. I'm sure hoping you'll be here when we start class next time."

How did you feel about the teacher's remarks this time?

_____

_____

_____

_____

Did the teacher blame you the second time or just explain how he felt about it? Which time did the teacher seem to care about you? Which time did you feel more like making a remark to get back at him?

The first message was a "You Message." The teacher blamed and accused *you* several times by saying, "'you" this and "you" that. He started each sentence with the word, "you." People who have the power to avoid unnecessary conflicts and settle conflicts they *are* in easily and quickly, never or rarely deliver "You Messages" because they know that it will make the other person feel angry, hurt, and up for a fight. They know that blaming never helps. They also realize that even if the person they deliver a "You Message" to doesn't say anything back at the time she is likely to get even in some way later.

The second message was an "I Message." The teacher told you how he felt and why. Both sentences were started with the word, "I."

Here's the formula:

1. I feel ...
2. when you ... (or that you...)
3. because...
4. What I need/want from you ... (or hoping you'll do) is...

It takes courage to use an "'I Message" because when you do it you are talking about yourself--your feelings and your wishes. You aren't placing blame on someone else.

Using an "'I Message" is a smart way to talk to people when you are frustrated by something they have done. With an "I Message" you express your own concerns. In order to express them, you have to be honest with yourself and recognize what your concerns are. When the listener hears your "I Message" she knows she has done something you object to, or feel bad about. By delivering an "I Message" you can make a strong, assertive statement without making the listener feel blamed which no one likes, even when guilty.

This is a clear way to tell people how you feel and what you want and need from them without causing them to want to get even. It's a great conflict management strategy!

Now it's your turn! Think of a situation involving another person that is bothering you and plan an "I Message" to say to him or her in order to assert yourself and avoid a destructive, unnecessary conflict at the same time. (In fact, after you deliver the message it may clear the air and bring about a favorable outcome for both of you.)

Write your "I Message" here:

_____
_____
_____
_____
_____
_____
_____
_____

As soon as you try this write about the experience:

_____
_____
_____
_____
_____
_____
_____
_____

Active Listening

We looked at how important listening is in Chapter Three. Here's another strategy that uses it. Have you noticed how you feel when you are upset about something and the other person, or people, involved won't listen? It just makes things worse. The opposite is also true: one of the best ways to settle a tense situation with someone is to listen. Just stop talking and start listening. To do it right you have to be respectful, sincere and silent no matter how much you want to say something. When you use this strategy you lean forward, look into the person's eyes, and really try to understand him, especially his feelings and opinions. Just keep listening and finally he will be ready to listen to you. But it will be awhile so be very, very patient. You may think that this strategy weakens your position, but guess again. It strengthens you. And, it works like a charm!

As soon as you try this write about the experience:

_____

_____

_____

_____

_____

Compromising

Let's say an impossible situation has presented itself: you and another person both want the same thing at the same time. So you suggest a compromise that allows each of you to get some of it. You could share something like a sandwich, or take turns using something like a computer. The way you use this strategy is to offer to give up something if the other person will do the same. The key is that *you* make the offer and *you* show that you will give up your part first. This almost always causes the other person to want to cooperate. If the thing you both want can't be divided or if the other person refuses to compromise, suggest flipping a coin.

As soon as you try this write about the experience:

_____

_____

_____

_____

_____

_____

Postponing

Have you ever noticed how fights usually happen when one, or both, people are in a bad mood, hungry, or tired? The strategy of postponing is exactly that--you suggest that you put off discussing the matter and get back to it later. You could say, "Look, Karla, I've had a long day and I feel lousy. Could we get back to this tomorrow?" Or "I've got an idea. Let's go eat and talk about this afterward. I'm so starved I can't think straight. What about you?" Do be sure to get back with her later at the agreed-upon time and then start out with active listening.

68

As soon as you try this write about the experience:

_____

_____

_____

_____

_____

_____

Apologizing and/or Expressing Regret

Sometimes a sincere apology and admitting your mistake is the best strategy when you have actually offended someone and they have become angry as anyone would. But there are times when you didn't say, or do, exactly what they think you said, or did. Let's suppose you say something and someone takes it the wrong way. Tell the person so as soon as you realize he or she is hurt or angry. Then have the strength to say you're sorry and explain that you never meant to cause bad feelings. Accidents are another example. You may have caused an accident somehow, but you never intended anyone to get hurt. That's when you might prefer to express regret. You could say, "It's terrible that it happened. I don't blame you for being mad" or "I'm sorry it happened. I didn't do it on purpose. Here, let me help." When other people know you feel regret, and that you care about them, it makes a huge difference.

As soon as you try this write about the experience:

_____

_____

_____

_____

_____

_____

Problem Solving

Sometimes things can get complicated between you and another person. With the strategy of problem solving you use as many of the other strategies as you can

69

especially active listening, I messages, and a calm, respectful voice. If you don't understand the other person, don't interrupt. When he finishes talking explain that you don't understand and ask questions. Then listen some more. Next, see if you can define the problem without any blaming. Take the attitude that the two of you are against the problem, not against each other. Suggest brainstorming ideas for solutions to the problem together and then agree on one, or more, that seem to make the most sense. If you can't agree on a solution, postpone deciding until later after each of you has had a chance to calm down and think about it some more.

What strategy would *you* use?

Read the following descriptions of conflicts. Then decide what strategy (or strategies) to use for each one.

Dan and Stan:

Dan and Stan are 16 year-old twins. Both are learning to drive. They are in a conflict about which one will get to drive with their dad for an hour before dinner. They have both finished their homework. Their dad is home but has to go out to a meeting after dinner. Dinner is in one hour.

If you were Dan, Stan, or their dad, what strategy (or strategies) would you use to manage this situation?

_____

_____

_____

Ellen and David:

Ellen and David have recently been married and things have been fine until spring brought good weather. But now Ellen is feeling resentful and hurt because David has preferred to spend much more time during the weekends on the golf course with his friends than he has chosen to spend at home with her. She thinks it's fine for him to have a sport but feels he's overdoing it. She is lonely for his company and David doesn't have a clue.

What strategy (or strategies) would you use to manage this situation if you were Ellen?

_____

_____

_____

Jim and Barbara:

Jim and Barbara are co-workers. They have been given a project to do cooperatively but cannot decide who will perform which tasks. All the other teams have begun work but Jim and Barbara are stuck. Both of them are becoming more annoyed with each other as the due date for their report to the CEO gets closer and closer.

What strategy (or strategies) would you use to manage this situation if you were Jim or Barbara?

_____

_____

_____

Julia and her mom:

Julia comes home from work to find her mom who has been babysitting her children very upset about something that all the "kids" in the family have done, including Julia. She tries to figure out what her children did and what she did, but it isn't clear. Her mom just keeps going on and on about how "all of you just keep messing up and making my life a misery." Julia is starting to feel frustrated and impatient.

If you were Julia what strategy (or strategies) would you use to manage this situation?

_____

_____

_____

Vinnie and Alex:

Vinnie and Alex are in the high school cafeteria heading for a table after filling their trays with food. Vinnie is following Alex and accidentally trips. This upsets Vinnie because he will have to go back for more food. But it upsets Alex more because his trousers got splashed with some very red spaghetti sauce. Alex starts to yell at Vinnie calling him a klutz.

If you were Vinnie, what strategy (or strategies) would you use to manage this situation?

_____

_____

_____

Ed Tyler and J.R. Johnson:

Ed Tyler and J.R. Johnson are both teachers in a middle school and they both teach six classes. They are on a committee to plan a carnival at the school. One day neither of them gets to eat lunch because of problems they had to handle during lunch period. They had agreed a few days ago to meet with each other that afternoon after school to discuss plans for the carnival. Unfortunately both men are tired and hungry. As they talk they discover that neither one likes any of the suggestions the other one makes. They can't seem to agree on anything and both of them are becoming irritable.

If you were Ed or J.R. what strategy (or strategies) would you use to manage this situation?

_____

_____

_____

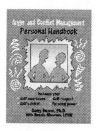

HOMEWORK: If you left any blanks in this chapter go back and read the questions again. Then fill in as many blanks as you can. Some of the questions ask what happened when you tried a particular conflict management strategy. Don't forget to try the strategies whenever opportunities arise. Then go back and write about what happened.

LIFE WORK: Be alert to how people around you, and in movies, react when provoked. Notice whether they behave aggressively, submissively, or assertively. Make a conscious effort to be assertive whenever possible. Remember assertiveness begins with your mind state (self-talk) and comes out in your words and deeds.

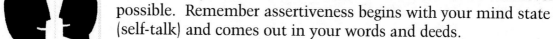

Don't be discouraged if you fall into aggressive or submissive behavior when you become upset. Just make it a point to keep trying to be assertive instead. Another point: don't be discouraged if your assertive actions don't work miracles. In some situations one assertive statement or action will have very little effect. In those situations it takes repeated assertive statements and actions to make a difference. Sometimes when you do something differently than what others expect they will try even harder to provoke you to act the way you acted in the past. Don't fall for it. Stick with the assertive program. It will eventually pay off.

"I never met a man I didn't like," stated Will Rogers in one of his monologues.

Upon hearing this as a youngster I reacted on two levels. "What about women?" was the first. But then, grasping the statement's power (Reaction #2) I decided Will must have meant he liked males and females alike. Inspired, I asked myself if I could possibly find something to like in everyone I met including generally unlikable people. Life gave me the opportunity to find out shortly thereafter.

It happened years ago but I clearly remember each moment of the entire episode. I was a small, physically underdeveloped, freckly blonde seventh grader in an ethnically mixed, inner city California junior high school. A verbally prolific little kid, I had the unfortunate habit of getting into trouble for saying things without thinking or at least looking around first to find out who might be listening.

Yolanda, a Latina classmate, was classically beautiful and developed to a fault. She had jet-black hair, olive skin, red-black lipstick, crucifix earrings, and lots of makeup. Everywhere she went four girls of similar appearance with whom she engaged in a clever mix of Spanish and English accompanied her. Their partially understandable conversation was punctuated with occasional bursts of sardonic laughter. Tantalized, I deeply wanted to be Yolanda's friend but her attitude toward my overtures was disdainful. She scowled at my friends and me if she looked at us at all.

One day toward the end of the second semester I confided to a friend that I didn't like Yolanda. I was unaware of being overheard by one of her allies. To my horror Yolanda approached me shortly afterward during fifth period and scathingly announced that she and I would "have it out" after school. "Meet me by the tunnel," she sneered. "Be alone and don't even think about not showing up!" Her friends were beside her snickering and adding insults.

I was practically paralyzed with terror over the next two hours. Word spread among the students about the upcoming event and I heard bits and pieces of conversations where bets were being made about how bad I would "get it." My friends felt sorry for me but were visibly relieved that Yolanda demanded I show up at the tunnel alone. A teacher caught wind of what was happening and, taking me to a private room, asked what she could do to help. That did it. I sobbed without shame and thanked her. I explained, however, that I had to face the ordeal alone or I would really get killed.

At the dismissal bell I walked out of the building into a throng of kids jeering in English and Spanish who followed me as I walked toward the tunnel like a prisoner to her execution. Suddenly, Yolanda appeared with her friends and stopped me on the sidewalk when I was about halfway there. Apparently she wanted to begin the confrontation where the widest possible audience could look on. There wouldn't be much room for a crowd in the tunnel.

Yolanda began by calling me a stupid little sh_ _ with a big mouth. Looking at the ground and humiliated to the core I nodded and everyone laughed. Next, she grabbed my collar and made me look at her. "You don't like me because I'm Mexican," she announced loudly. An ominous rumbling growl issued from the crowd.

Instantly I protested in a stronger voice

than I expected myself to generate: "No! No, that's not true." And then I shocked everyone, especially myself, by blurting, "That is *not* why I don't like you!"

Seconds of silence that seemed like forever followed and then Yolanda shrieked, "What? You admit it?" Then she shoved me toward the tunnel and hissed, "Okay, you asked for it. Get going."

Suddenly hooting and laughter erupted. I heard a boy's voice say, "Hey, Yolanda? You hear that? Who can blame her?" Another said, "Oh man, she tells the truth!" One other taunted, "Ay, Yolanda, posible tiene razon!" (Maybe she has a reason.) Others were out for blood: "Give it to her, Yoli!" and "Que pega la pendeja." (Just hit the idiot.)

Yolanda gripped my arm as she forced me down the stairs into the urine-stenched narrow pit that ran from one side of the boulevard to the other. Every kid who could find a toehold around us crowded in. Yolanda screamed at them to back off to give her some room and began to circle me like a hungry wolf. To my surprise she repeated, "You don't like me because I'm Mexican. That's why you don't like any of us." Once again the crowd reacted with a hateful growl.

A deep sadness overcame me. I was quivering inside but looking her straight in the eye I said, "I was stupid to say what I said so loudly that your friend heard me. I never wanted you to hear it. But you being Mexican isn't why I said it."

Yolanda objected again. "Tell the truth. You don't like Mexicans!" and again I denied it by shaking my head firmly.

"Okay, tell her why you don't like her," someone shouted. "Yeah, gringita, tell her the truth," came another voice.

"Shut up!" Yolanda screamed and her friends gave the crowd menacing looks. But they persisted: "Yeah. Tell her. Do it! Do it!"

I was not relieved by any of this. All I wanted to do was either die on the spot or be magically transported out of there. What to do? Being outnumbered, I would be a fool to fight back when she attacked me. (I could see where boys in situations like these are in even worse binds.) I looked at Yolanda and realized that in a far more serious way she too was miserable. I took a deep breath, held her gaze, and quietly said, "You aren't friendly. At the beginning of the year I tried to make friends with you but you never said 'Hi' when I said 'Hi' and when I smiled at you, you never smiled back. I liked you a lot at first, but then I gave up."

At this point one of Yolanda's friends snarled, "Give it to her, Yoli," but Yoli was frozen in space staring at me and after a few moments I continued: "You think I don't like Mexicans but you're wrong. You want the truth? I would love to have your hair and your skin. And I wish I could speak two languages like you, and I'm sorry that I hurt your feelings."

Yolanda listened and her eyes grew larger. She seemed to be amazed, then suddenly swallowed, shook herself, and sneered, "Well look who's kissing my ass!"

At this point my humiliation was overwhelming and I looked at the floor of the tunnel waiting for whatever would happen next.

"Get away from me," she screamed. "Just get out of here." Without looking at anyone Yolanda gestured at the crowd to part and let me climb the steps. Surprised, but eager to get away as fast as I could, I rushed up the stairs and ran across the boulevard after quickly checking the flow of traffic. Thank God a bus going my way was taking on passengers on the other side. I hurriedly climbed aboard, showed the driver my pass and found a seat. Instantly I was overcome with racking sobs. Without looking at anyone I used my dress to sop up torrents of tears.

The end of the term came soon. Terrified of Yolanda, I carefully avoided her. There were no confrontations, not even eye contact. Summer came and went. When school started again in September something happened that still puzzles me: I was seated in a classroom as Yolanda entered. We spied each other but before I could avert my gaze she smiled, and cheerily said, "Hi girl, how've you been?" I literally looked behind me and seeing no one looked back supposing she was baiting me for another confrontation. But Yolanda, keeping her distance, kept smiling an apparently sincere smile. "Did you have a good summer?" she asked. But I was too shocked to respond. During the rest of our eighth grade year Yolanda, who no longer hung out with her former friends, went out of her way to greet me with a warm smile. I was still so freaked out that I rarely responded with a fraction of her friendly energy but it didn't seem to matter to her. The next year Yolanda did not attend our school and I don't know what happened to her.

I never found out what caused the change in Yolanda and I don't take credit for the massive transformation she demonstrated. Clearly, over the summer something or someone helped her resolve the inner conflict that spurred her destructive actions. Yolanda's friendliness to me the next year was simply an extension of this resolution but the fact that she consistently made a deliberate effort to reach out to me said something. As I've pondered what happened through the years

I've concluded that telling her the truth-- how her behavior caused me to give up on being friends and what it was that I *did* like about her--may have been a factor in her growth.

As horrific the incident and puzzling the aftermath, it has served me. I am particularly sensitive to the pain of people who are bullied for whatever reason and for the perpetrators themselves. With a certain confidence I have dedicated my career to helping people overcome their inner barriers and my personal life to overcoming my own. I *know* healing and transformation can happen because at a tender age Yolanda proved it to me.

Chapter Five:
More Anger and Conflict Management Strategies

In the second, third and fourth chapters we talked about ways people act when angry. Some of these actions create disharmony and others create harmony. Specifically, in Chapter Two we looked at hurtful, anger-driven things family members sometimes do to each other at home. In Chapter Three we focused on non-verbal and verbal communication including both destructive and constructive ways to communicate with others. In Chapter Four we talked about the advantages of being assertive instead of behaving aggressively or submissively. We also looked at several conflict management strategies in Chapter Four.

Here is a list of actions described in Chapters Two, Three and Four. Draw a check mark by the actions listed below that you recently noticed another person doing. Draw an X next to the ones you did yourself:

_____ Unconscious imitation
_____ Acting out
_____ Displacement
_____ Scapegoating
_____ Eye contact
_____ Withholding eye contact
_____ Smiling
_____ Scowling
_____ Interrupting
_____ Aggressive behavior
_____ Submissive behavior
_____ Assertive behavior
_____ Apologizing and/or expressing regret

_____ Probing
_____ Dominating
_____ Judging
_____ Giving unasked-for advice
_____ Putting down / name calling
_____ Misinterpreting
_____ Accusing / Criticizing
_____ Stating an I message
_____ Listening with the third ear
_____ Compromising
_____ Postponing
_____ Problem solving
_____ Active listening

Pick one of the actions you noticed another person do that was destructive, unhelpful or provoking. Describe it and how it affected you:

_____

_____

_____

_____

Pick one of the actions you did yourself that was constructive and helpful. Describe it and how it seemed to affect the person(s) you were involved with:

_____

_____

_____

_____

_____

How did it make you feel about yourself?

_____

_____

_____

_____

How you feel about yourself is very important!

Anger management brings good results! The more you observe yourself and decide to carefully *choose* your actions, especially when you are stressed or angry, the more you will respect yourself. The more you respect yourself through self-control, the more true positive personal power you possess. This is the path to genuine satisfaction and happiness even if the other people you are in contact with are clueless and out of control.

It bears repeating: none of us can fully control anyone except ourselves! (Many times that's a handful.) Flying off the handle is easy. It can happen before you even know it. The period of time between the moment your button gets pushed and the action you take is "the critical interval." What you do in that interval results in how you act, or react, followed by how you feel about yourself afterward!

Let's go over the path to self-respect and positive personal power one more time:

- First, you allow yourself to know what you're feeling, even if it's unpleasant.
- Second, you *decide* to control your impulse to fight or take flight, perhaps using chilling out strategies (more on this later).
- Next, as soon as you can think clearly, you consider options for what to do.
- Then you *decide* on the best assertive option that will not create pain for anyone, including you.
- Finally, you act assertively and continue to do so.

When the going really gets tough--what should you do?

The rest of this chapter offers suggestions for strategies you can use in particularly difficult situations that could cost you dearly if you let anger, fear, or insecurity get the better of you. These strategies are geared to help you stay safe and handle yourself. After you read the description of each strategy, you may write notes to yourself in response to the questions that are asked.

Keep in mind that every person and situation are different and "judgement calls" need to be made. What works in one situation with one person, or group, might not work in another. If you have been experiencing extreme feelings of fear, emotional pain and/or rage due to frightening, hurtful and/or unjust situations, talk with other people you trust--a counselor, your pastor, a teacher, a family member or a friend to hear their ideas.

Arm Yourself Mentally!

Why is it that some people seem strong and rarely get picked on while others seem to be the victim over and over again? The ones who seem strong might not even be very big or physically strong, but they seem to be protected in some way. Frequent victims might be large people and physically strong, but it almost seems like they are wearing a sign that says, "Hit me."

Are some people really protected while others are not? Yes! But their protection is not a weapon, nor is it magic. It's just the way they think and feel about themselves. They are confident and in control of themselves *and they know it*. They trust in their own ability to handle situations, even tough ones. Their confident thoughts and feelings show in their assertive manner and actions--what they say and do--even the way they walk! Bullies rarely pick these people to mess with because it's so much easier and more fun to torment the ones who are not confident.

The protection of inner strength and confidence is available to everyone. You can have it too. If you don't feel confident inside, you can teach it to yourself. Just like physical exercise to make your body strong, you can do mental exercises to make your personality strong. *In fact, professional athletes do both!*

The foundation for becoming assertive and being protected is "mental training" in which you think positive thoughts about yourself and imagine yourself with an impenetrable metal shield around you that causes threats and mean words to bounce off. Never, ever put yourself down out loud or in your thoughts. If you catch yourself doing it, turn the thought around. If you say, *"I'm so dumb,"* to yourself, say, *"I'm SO smart,"* to correct it. In fact, say things like *"I'm safe" "I'm okay" "I'm valuable"* to yourself many times each day.

Here are some other positive thoughts you can train yourself to think and believe about yourself. Say them frequently:

> *"I can handle any problem."*
> *"When the going gets tough, I always know what to do."*
> *"I can calm down and breathe when I feel upset."*
> *"I trust myself."*
> *"I care about people and they care about me."*

One word of caution: don't overdo it and come off arrogant. That invites people to want to bring you down.

After you have done this for a period of time, like one week, write yourself some notes about it:

_____

_____

_____

_____

_____

CHILL YOURSELF OUT!

Most hostility and violence happens because at least one person is extremely angry, unable to think straight, got out of control, and acted on impulse. It's a chain reaction that often leads to pain and regret. *Don't be that person!*

You can't stop yourself from getting extremely angry or scared at times. That's normal. It's also normal to feel like striking back or running away from whoever made you mad. But that's *not* being strong; it's the opposite. It takes great strength and self-control to stop yourself from fighting or taking flight and when you do it, you give yourself a big advantage. The fact is that it's hard to think when you're upset, but think you must for things to work out right. That's why you need to chill yourself out first.

Here are some strategies you can use when you are extremely angry to calm yourself down and regain control of yourself:

Breathe! Are you aware that whenever people become tense they practically stop breathing? This isn't good because when oxygen to the brain is reduced it's hard to think. You go blank and that only makes you feel worse. It also makes it easier for your impulses to take over. So, when you are upset, tell yourself to breathe. Take deep breaths--lots of them. You'll notice a difference soon in how you feel. Your ability to think and handle yourself will return. You will get in touch with your *real* strength.

Count! Count to ten. Thomas Jefferson made this suggestion and it has worked for millions of people for two centuries. There are alternatives: you could count backwards from 100 by tens, or to 100 by fives. Breathe deeply at the same time. When you try this you'll find it keeps your impulses under control. Afterward you will be more able to think straight.

Use words that suit you. Instead of counting some people prefer to say things to themselves while they breathe deeply. Try saying: *"You're cool"* ... *"Chill out now"* ... *"You're in control"* ... *"Re – lax"* or whatever works for you.

If you feel like you're about to explode no matter how hard you try to calm yourself, do it in such a way that you won't complicate things further. Scream into a pillow. Punch a mattress. Go for a hard run. Go somewhere completely private and talk out loud to yourself about your feelings. Find a friend you trust and talk it out or see a counselor. These people can be very helpful at times like this.

If you have tried some of these ideas when you were feeling extremely angry, write about how you chilled yourself out and then what happened:

_____

_____

_____

_____

_____

Consider the Consequences

When people in prison are asked, *"What do you want to say to people outside, especially kids?"* their answer is almost always the same: *"Think about the consequences of what you are about to do before you do it. DON'T assault someone, pick a fight, take a bully's bait, shoot, drive drunk, take drugs, steal, take unfair advantage of someone, threaten, talk bad about people behind their backs, or put somebody down UNTIL YOU STOP AND THINK ABOUT WHAT COULD HAPPEN IF YOU DO IT."*

This is their answer because they have had many months and years to think about what they did and wish they had stopped themselves and done some rational thinking before they did it. Not only are they locked up in a terrible place, many prisoners have to live knowing they caused other people to suffer horribly--victims they purposely attacked, or those who were hurt, or even killed, because they accidentally got in the way. Other victims are the people who grieve for friends and family members who were hurt.

What causes people to act without considering the consequences?

- Extreme anger coupled with the urge to get even. (This is the big one for "crimes of passion" that are driven by hate and anger.)
- Not being able to refuse temptations that are unhealthy or unsafe.
- Enjoying the thrill of feeling powerful by bullying or baiting someone.
- Losing contact with reality and the ability to use good judgement by abusing alcohol or drugs.
- Folding to "peer pressure" and taking a dare, or going along with the group in an action that leads to trouble.
- Being afraid to take a stand when something unjust is happening.

These reasons have caused painful outcomes for all kinds of people, including: the end of a relationship, a referral to an authority, paying a stiff fine, being ordered to make restitution, even being sentenced to jail or prison. These reasons have also resulted in suicide, trauma, unwanted pregnancy, poverty, and fear.

Consequences like these are never planned. Few people get up in the morning and decide to purposely mess up their lives or the lives of others. But when their actions lead to terrible consequences many act bewildered and ask, "*How did this happen?*" They often give excuses or blame what they "had to do" on someone else. But the truth is that they made it happen themselves. If they are honest with themselves they know it's true. It's also true that the outcomes of their actions probably wouldn't have happened if, at first, they had found the courage to stop and consider the consequences.

When have you had the strength to stop yourself from a destructive action and considered the consequences first?

_____

_____

_____

_____

_____

How to Respond to Verbal Assault

One of the most difficult spots to find yourself in is when someone intends to insult you and put you down by making cruel remarks--maliciously teasing and tormenting you with words that hurt and make you furious. It's especially bad if you are verbally assaulted in front of other people.

This kind of situation is tough to manage skillfully for two reasons. First, you need to deal with your own strong feelings and not let the person get the better of you. Second, you have to respond to your attacker in such a way that you don't lose face while at the same time causing him or her to decide that the attack isn't worth it.

Why do people verbally attack other people? It's important to know their two main motives:

- Verbal attackers don't feel very good about themselves (even though they may act like they do). For this reason they give in to the urge to put others down in the belief that it builds *them* up.

- Verbal attackers want to intimidate. They believe their intimidating words will give them social power, control, and dominance over you and other people who see the attack or hear about it.

How should you respond? Generally, to manage your anger, you must do two things when you are the victim of verbal assault.

Self-control comes first so that your response is within your full command. If you aren't in control of yourself your response is likely to miss the mark and make things worse. Many people feel like answering a verbal assault with a physical assault. That's a normal impulse, but where will it lead? Trouble *for you!* Other people feel like getting away immediately but that tells attackers they "won" encouraging them to attack you all the more. You will also look like a coward to anyone watching.

Get control of yourself by breathing deeply, straightening your body to your full height and telling yourself that you can handle this. Then, using every bit of strength in your personality, look straight at your attacker and make a strong comeback. Continue to breathe deeply, don't blink, and get ready to speak.

Fit your words to your attacker's motive.

- If you think your attacker wants to feel better about him/herself by putting you down, look at him or her and firmly say something like: "Do you really think saying that to me builds *you* up?"

83

- If you think your attacker is trying to achieve power, control, and dominance over you, make a strong stand. While staring at him or her firmly say something like: "You don't scare me. I see what you're trying to do and I don't care *what* you think about (my sister, my weight, my hair, my height--whatever the attack was about)."

You may have to respond more than once. Sometimes when people don't get the reaction they want they try harder. In other words, they get worse before they get better. So get ready. Do the same posture with your body, stare at your attacker and say, "I told you before... (then repeat the same statement you made the first time). You may feel like a broken record, saying the same thing again and again, but do it anyway. It works.

Remember, you do not deserve to be attacked. No one does. Don't back down. (Refer also to the strategies for responding to extreme hostility and to bullies.)

Have you tried these strategies in a situation where someone verbally assaulted you? If so, write about the experience:

_____

_____

_____

_____

How to Respond to Extreme Hostility

Another very difficult situation is when a person is extremely hostile and seems on the verge of physical violence. There could be lots of different reasons the person is so worked up. Perhaps you seriously offended him or her. Whether the reason makes sense or not the person's hostility *is potentially dangerous. The most important thing to consider in this situation is your safety.*

Here are some suggestions to avoid becoming a victim of physical violence, and possibly, to defuse the person's hostility:

- Stay cool. Don't do anything at first except breathe deeply. This gives you time to think.
- Look at the person calmly and keep breathing. Don't show fear and don't argue or try to explain anything. Extremely angry people can't hear a word you're saying. If you argue it will inflame *not defuse* the person and violence may result.
- Back off, keeping eye contact. Hold up your head but keep a plain expression.

Or, before backing off, you might decide to try to understand and communicate with the hostile person. If so,

- Calmly ask, "I can see that you are very upset. Tell me what's wrong."
- Then listen and listen some more. Let the person know you understand by repeating in an even voice what you heard him or her say. (For example: "You're angry because I bumped into you.")
- No matter how unreasonable you believe the person is being, sincerely express regret and concern. (For example: "Oh, I see what you mean. It's too bad that happened.") If it's appropriate, apologize.
- Stop talking and let the person make the next move. By now the person will probably feel less hostile if he or she believes you understand and care.
- If the person is still hostile, back off, keeping eye contact. Hold up your head but keep a plain expression.

(Refer also to the strategies for responding to verbal assault and to bullies.)

Have you tried these strategies in a situation where a hostile person seemed on the verge of violence? If so, write about the experience:

_____

_____

_____

_____

How to Respond to a Bully

What do bullies want? They want respect but will settle for attention, control, or fear. Bullies may seem strong and scary but it's all an act. They are trying to convince you that they could do you damage, *but mainly they are trying to convince themselves.* Inside, bullies feel anything but strong. By controlling, scaring, and hurting other people they fool themselves into thinking they are proving their strength.

Bullies act like they can damage you because they have been damaged or imagine that they have been damaged. They may have been victims of bad treatment probably as small children. Many were abused and may not remember it. Some still live with abusive people in their homes or neighborhoods. Being hurt, or imagining they have been hurt, causes some people to want to hurt back usually not caring who it is. Some have never learned to control themselves but they want to control you and believe you "owe" them your allegiance.

Bullies want to feel powerful so badly they don't play fair. They may tease or bait you by calling you names or calling someone you care about names. They might accuse you of being (scared, dumb, ugly, chicken, gay, whatever) or take something from you but only when they have the advantage like when they are in a group of bullies or if they have a weapon. Bullies hit below the belt any way they can to sucker you into a fight you are unlikely to win. They do it to get a power high.

Obviously, rule #1 is to stay as far away from bullies as you can. However, when an episode occurs and the deck is stacked against you, what can you do to end it without becoming a victim and without groveling? Here are some suggestions:

- First and foremost: Don't take the bait! This means don't argue, trade insults, or try to seriously reason with a bully.
- Breathe and gaze calmly at the bully. *Don't show fear.* If the bully demands you give him or her your money or something else, hold your dignity and say something like: "Aw come on, (Jack). You're no thief."
- Slowly walk away keeping eye contact and a tall posture.

Three other ideas:

- Agree. (Imagine the bully has just called you stupid. Your response, perhaps with a smile: "Yep. You may be right. But I do my best.") Then walk away, keeping eye contact.
- Give them what they want. If more than one grabs one of your belongings and throws it back and forth baiting you to try to get it, don't. Just say, "If you like it so much, you can have it." This ends the game and they are likely to throw the item where you can get it later. If it's outright theft, let the bully and your property go. Report the theft to the authorities if you believe it's safe to do so.
- Don't physically fight a bully, or anyone, unless you have been physically attacked and your response is to defend yourself. Unfortunately, this is the only language some bullies understand.

(Refer also to the strategies for responding to verbal assault and extreme hostility.)

Have you tried these strategies when someone bullied you? If so, write about the experience:

_____

_____

_____

_____

_____

How to Respond to Peer Pressure

To "just say no" when someone, or a group, is pressuring you to do something you don't want to do isn't easy for most people. "Peer pressure" doesn't just happen to children and teens, it can happen to you at any time in your life.

Let's imagine a scenario involving peer pressure that is happening to a married adult and consider some ideas for handling it. (The pressuring aspects of this situation are similar to those faced by people at any age.)

Scenario: Your friends know your spouse and children are going out of town for the weekend and they want to come to your house for a party. You know they have some serious booze and they plan to bring it. They also plan to invite some people who like to have sex at parties. You can foresee a bad scene including damage to your house and your spouse's anger. How do you let your friends know you don't want to go along with the plan without having them reject you?

Ask questions such as: "You mean you want me to open my house to that crowd?" "Aren't they the ones who trashed Walter's place on July 4th?" "You want me to take a risk like that?" Questions of this kind usually show the people pressuring you how unreasonable their demands are. After asking each question stop talking and wait to hear the response. Chances are they will realize you're not going to be submissive. This may cause them to back off.

Reconsider your friendships with people who are inconsiderate! *Are they really your friends?*

If you decide you can't end your relationship with people who pressure you in these ways, you will have to handle the pressure. If you were the married adult who doesn't want the party, you could give an excuse. For example, you could tell them your mother-in-law (or some other non-drinking relative) is going to spend the weekend at your house while your spouse is gone. No way can the party happen then. Or explain that your neighbors see everything and report it. Let them know your spouse will find out for sure and that won't be pretty.

Let's say your friends accept what you told them but now they want you to go to a similar party somewhere else. You aren't interested but they keep pressuring you to join in. This may be when you must finally explain: "I really like hanging out with you guys. We do a lot of things together that I want to keep doing but that kind of party just isn't my thing. I hope you can accept that." You may have to take this position more than once.

Finally, Be assertive and stand your ground: Be true to yourself. If your friends won't leave you alone and keep putting on the pressure this may be the time to just say no and say it firmly.

Have you reconsidered some of your friendships or tried these kinds of strategies for handling peer pressure? If so, write about those experiences:

_____

_____

_____

_____

Resolve Problems with Mediation

Mediation is a process that is being used more and more in practically every community in many nations to resolve conflicts. It's much less expensive and painful than legal action and is occurring in schools, agencies, companies and court-related settings. In fact, even nations that otherwise might go to war are sometimes solving their problems through mediation.

Here's how it works: Let's say two individuals are in a heated dispute with one another. The dispute could be about anything. The mediator meets with them in a private place where they work on the problem with the mediator's help until a solution both individuals can live with has been reached. The mediator calls the shots.

Here's the process in a nutshell:
- First, the mediator gets both people to agree to these rules:
    - Whatever we say here is private--it stays in this room.
    - There will be no interruptions, name calling, put downs, or fighting.
    - When it's your turn to speak, be as honest as you can.
    - Agree to find a resolution to the conflict.
- Second, the mediator gives each person a turn to tell the other what he or she did that made him or her angry.
- Third, the mediator makes sure that each person heard the other correctly by having them take turns telling each other what they heard each other say.
- Fourth, the mediator has each person take a turn telling the other what he or she wants the other to do differently that would solve the problem for him or her.
- Fifth, the mediator continues to help the people come up with more ideas they both can agree on in order to solve the problem. This continues until at least one idea for a solution that both people are satisfied with has been reached.
- Last, the mediator has both people write down the solution using the exact same words. Both sign each other's paperwork.

- Finally, the people are asked to shake hands before leaving.

Have you been involved in mediation? If so, write yourself some notes about the experience. Or, if you have a dispute with someone that needs solving write some notes to yourself about how mediation might help.

_____

_____

_____

_____

_____

 **HOMEWORK:** Many of the strategies in this chapter address situations you may have experienced in the past and/or may experience in the future. The situations may not be ones you are experiencing now. Remember to come back to this handbook and refer to it when conflicts arise in your life and you are feeling angry. This will refresh your memory of helpful strategies you can use.

LIFE WORK: Strive to continue being self-observant, self-respecting, self-possessed, self-controlled, and assertive. Remember to allow others to be themselves by showing them respect and compassion.

Managing anger and conflict are lifelong challenges but worth doing.

The rewards are Self-Respect and Positive Personal Power!

Resources

Bilodeau, Lorraine, M.S. *The Anger Workbook,* Center City, MN: Hazeldon Information & Educational Services, 1992.

Dunne, Gerry, Ph.D. *Preventing Violence in Our Schools: Classroom Activities and Strategies for Teachers and Counselors,* (Second Edition), Carson, CA: Jalmar Press, 2002.

Dunne, Gerry, Ph.D. Reverend Paul Tuchardt and Caroline Tuchardt. *A Christian Perspective on Violence Prevention: Manual for Youth Leaders and Christian Educators* (companion to the Guide, above), Carson CA: Jalmar Press, 2000.

Dunne, Gerry, Ph.D., Reverend Paul Tuchardt and Caroline Tuchardt, with a foreword by Reverend Richard L. Schaefer. *A Catholic Perspective on Violence Prevention: Manual for Youth Leaders and Catholic Educators* (companion to the Guide, above), Carson CA: Jalmar Press, 2002.

Dunne, Gerry, Ph.D. *The Close Call: How Can You Stop Violence Before It Starts?* (a booklet for teens), Carson CA: Jalmar Press, 2002.

Elgin, Suzette Haden. *The Gentle Art of Verbal Self-Defense,* Dorset Press, 1980.

Goleman, Daniel. *Emotional Intelligence: Why It Can Matter More Than IQ,* New York: Bantam Books, 1995.

Horn, Sam. *Tongue Fu,* New York: St. Martin's Press, 1996.

Ruiz, Don Miguel. *The Four Agreements,* San Rafael, CA: Amber-Allen Publishing, 1997.

Tavris, Carol. *Anger: The Misunderstood Emotion,* New York: Simon & Schuster, 1982.